MW00776354

Untarnished

RECLAIMING MY SELF-WORTH THROUGH ── GOD'S ──
Untainted Love

DONNA S. FARRAR

Copyright © 2021 Donna S. Farrar

This is a work of nonfiction; however, many of the names, identifying details of the characters, and events, have been changed or modified.

Unless otherwise indicated, all Scripture quotations are taken from the Holy Bible, New Living Translation, copyright © 1996, 2004, 2015 by Tyndale House Foundation. Used by permission of Tyndale House Publishers, Inc., Carol Stream, Illinois 60188. All rights reserved. "Scripture quotations are from the ESV® Bible (The Holy Bible, English Standard Version®), copyright © 2001 by Crossway, a publishing ministry of Good News Publishers. Used by permission. All rights reserved." Scripture quotations from The Authorized (King James) Version. Rights in the Authorized Version in the United Kingdom are vested in the Crown. Reproduced by permission of the Crown's patentee, Cambridge University Press

All rights reserved. No part of this document may be reproduced or transmitted in any form or by any means, electronic, mechanical, photocopying, recording, or otherwise, without prior written permission of the author.

UNTARNISHED
Reclaiming My Self-Worth Through God's Untainted Love

Donna S. Farrar
Donna Sherrie, LLC
Po Box 1121, Garner, NC 27529
www.donnasherrie.com • contact@donnasherrie.com

ISBN 978-1-949826-37-1
Printed in the USA.
All rights reserved

Published by: EAGLES GLOBAL BOOKS | Frisco, Texas
In conjunction with the 2021 Eagles Authors Course
Cover & interior designed by DestinedToPublish.com

Dedication

For

My husband, my hero

Acknowledgments

I've wanted to write a book for a very long time, and I'm glad I finally had the courage to move from a spirit of fear to a spirit of power. I couldn't have finished this book without Holy Spirit, my husband for giving me the space and time, my writing coach who encouraged me every step of the way, and my editor and publisher.

Special thanks to the wonderful mothers in my life, Brenda N. and Kay F., for always checking in with me and holding me accountable by asking for book progress updates.

To my dad, Donald, who always believes in me no matter the obstacles.

To H. Kay Altman for loving me like her very own the first time we met and never stopping.

To my AWF church family.

To Eagles International Training Institute – thank you for making this opportunity possible.

And with indebted gratitude, to everyone who encouraged, genuinely loved and cared for me before, during, and after my time of incarceration. GOD, through using many of you, helped me to see my value, self-worth, and place in the kingdom of GOD. I love you always.

Contents

Introduction

Sentencing Day

WINTER OF '08

March 3, 2008, was finally here, after spending 520 days—nearly 17 months—in Davidson County Jail. One of the guards hollered my name: "Dixon, let's roll." I was headed to the courtroom downstairs before the judge to confirm the plea deal I had signed a few weeks prior. The plea deal was for 5 years and 10 months. This moment was terrifying and also exhilarating, because I was finally getting out of this dump and moving forward with my life. Of course, I didn't want to go to prison. In my mind, I could think of a million other places I would rather be.

I walked into the courtroom with orange and white stripes, a pair of flip-flops with socks, and my hair braided. There was no time to get ready or put on a nice fancy outfit, as that was certainly not allowed. I remember the judge reading my plea deal to me, informing me that I would receive time served (meaning the number of days already spent in jail would be credited toward my sentence) and wishing me good luck. I went back to B block and into my cell with no words. The fears of what prison would be like swelled up in my mind. I guess the officer who escorted me back could see what I was thinking on my face. She said to me, "Dixon, you're going to be okay. You're going to make it through this. Be strong, keep your head up, and your time will be over before you know it." I was surprised by the encouragement. Ms. S was considered one of the meanest officers at Davidson County Jail. She kept a straight face, treated everyone the same, and didn't put up with any mess. Early the next morning, I was transported to the primary women's prison in North Carolina, which housed over 1500 women.

Prior to sentencing day, my days in Davidson County Jail were long and unknown. I created paper calendars just to keep up with the passage of time. Each month, I would tally up the days I had already spent there on a sheet of paper. I used toothpaste as tape to stick my handmade paper calendar to the wet, moldy, Pepto-Bismol-pink-colored wall.. There were four women to every cell with a permanently smudged mirror, a sink, and a steel toilet without a lid or privacy. When we had to release our bowels, we used our personal blankets as shields. Each cell had two metal bunk beds on each side of the wall with thin, hunter green, twin-sized mattresses. The blue teddy bears displayed as wall art along the top edges of the wall provided no comfort. There was one old, cemented, carved-out, crusted, moldy shower for 16 women without any temperature adjustments. One day it was scorching hot, and another icy cold. The food was disgusting, always the same, and mysterious meat was served. (Of course, I wasn't expecting a gourmet meal.) The conditions alone were enough to persuade me that I wouldn't enjoy the stay. My bond was set at half a million dollars because I was supposedly considered a flight risk, even though I had no prior arrests or justice system involvement. It wasn't until several months later that the judge granted to lower my bond to $75,000—meaning if I could come up with 10% of that, then I would be on my way home—but financially it wasn't an option.

My first night inside was gut-wrenching. I sat on the bench where we ate our meals, holding a stone face so the other women couldn't size me up or sense my emotions. I knew they wanted to know what I was in for, but I kept to myself for some time until I got a decent inkling about some of them. For the next few weeks, I tried calling everyone whose numbers I knew by heart to help me get out of this dump. I could hear the sounds of pity in their voices as I told them where I had ended up. The most difficult call was the one I made to my mom. I could hear her anger and frustration at me for making such a poor decision. She was heartbroken and disappointed. I knew I had let her down. What was I going to do now? What would be the outcome of all this? How would I get myself out of this situation? So many thoughts ran through my mind, even suicidal ones at one point. At first, it was really hard to see a positive outcome; but, as time went on, and as I started spending time with God and dealing intricately with the inner me, I learned how to think positively and developed a new mindset.

The good part about being hundreds of miles away from my family and friends is that no one inside the jail knew me on a personal level. If I wanted to, I could pretend to be a hardcore drug dealer, a ride or die chick, a conformist to the environment, or I could just be plain ol' me—easygoing, nonchalant, and loyal to my circle. I chose the latter, as this was the simplest, and if I had thought to portray someone I wasn't, the girls on my block would certainly call me out, as they often did if they had known each other on the streets and crossed paths.

Once my inkling about a few of the girls settled in, Keisha, Shauna, and Toya made my waiting game a whole lot easier. Keisha had a loud, deep voice and constantly cracked jokes. Toya was always ready to fight and made sure everyone knew she liked men. And Shauna was so genuine and pure. She treated me like I was her little sister. She was the one I could relate to the most, because we had similar charges and shared experiences. Shauna encouraged me until the day she left to further complete her sentence in the penitentiary. Later on, I even received letters from her letting me know that she was doing okay and, of course, ready to go home.

To pass the time, I would read, play spades or Phase 10, sleep, write, and make collect calls. There was no physical library onsite, but we traded and shared books that women would leave or that would get sent in via mail. Playing spades,

Nay and I on the same team were no match for anyone against us. We were unstoppable. To sleep was a blessing, as I often had dreams of being back out in society and experiencing my physical freedom once again. Sometimes waking up from a dream was a bummer. Writing became my privilege. Weekly I wrote long letters to my loved ones, hoping they would quickly respond back to me, and I'm grateful they very often did. All the answered calls reminded me that I had family and friends who actually cared and prayed for me.

Monday nights became a highlight for me. Ms. Gail, Candace, and another group of ladies would come to visit at the jail. They would sing, teach, preach, pass out Bibles and Daily Bread pamphlets, provide holiday-acceptable gifts, and encourage us. With their encouragement, I felt like I could get through another week. I was given a Gideon Bible. I had never really read the Bible before, besides a few Psalms and Proverbs scriptures. I only knew the scriptures my dad taught me to memorize as a little girl: Colossians 3:20, *Children, obey your parents in all things, for this is well pleasing to the Lord,*" and Philippians 4:13, *"I can do all things through Christ who strengthens me"* (NKJV). And at this point in my life, I needed to know more. I wanted to read the Bible myself and understand it. I remember one of the volunteers recommending I start with the book of John, and I did.

This slow thought of transformation occurred after several months of being in jail. I didn't rededicate my life to Jesus just so I could somehow miraculously get out of jail (although that would have been nice). I realized how much turmoil I was in physically, mentally, spiritually, and emotionally. Regardless of what day the officer may have called my name to exit the jail, I wanted to be ready, bold enough, fierce enough, and self-controlled enough not to surrender to the same people, behaviors, and places that had led me here.

I had no interest in what some call jailhouse religion. I needed truth, and truth for me was found in the Word of God. I could never say that jail or prison saved my life, because it would be totally inaccurate. But what I can say is that God met me there, and I'm glad He didn't leave me nor forget about me. Walking through this storm allowed me to seek God to help deal with my brokenness, childhood trauma, unforgiveness, and so many other unaddressed aspects of my life. My journey of learning self-worth has been painful, uncomfortable, confusing, fretful, and unwarranted at times. Being in jail and eventually prison thrust me to intentionally regain my identity in Christ and ultimately see my worth in Him.

Chapter 1

The Shift

Street life behaviors come with residual repercussions.

SPRING '06

Everything appeared to be moving in the right direction. I was in my new one-bedroom apartment, recently renovated with full amenities. Definitely a hot commodity back in '06 for a 20-year-old young woman. No roommate, no cleaning up after anyone else or worrying about whether Ife would pay her half of the rent. I was on my own, officially independent, living in Baltimore City. It was the farthest south I had ever anticipated living, and only three hours from Jersey. My best friend Blue and I had decided to attend two different HBCUs in the heart of Baltimore. Eventually, she transferred to another HBCU in North Carolina, but I stayed. I got to know several people, learned how to get around town pretty well, and got to kick it with Shawn.

FALL '03

Shawn was well known throughout the city, but I didn't know that when I first met him. He attended the same HBCU prior to my arrival but hadn't finished for whatever personal reasons. The late summer night was dark, and I was heading back to my dorm from visiting my old roommate Drea. She and I met prior to the fall semester during early summer freshman orientation.

As I was crossing the circle where pickup and drop-off happened, I heard someone from a early '90s gold Honda Accord call out, "Hey, what's up, shorty?" I happened to look, and there I saw a light skinned, freckled nose, red goatee, long brown dreadlocks guy. Honestly, I don't remember the conversation in full detail, but I remember I was convinced by his looks alone that I should engage, that I should get in the car with this fine man and see what's up, and to be frank, I did just that. I got in the car and rode to a liquor store on West North Ave. The car stopped, and he hopped out to purchase some brown liquor. Whatever the brand was, I'd never had it before. It burned my throat, and I chased it down with some lemonade. I wanted to impress him.

That night, I got to experience the Baltimore nightlife. I glimpsed the Inner Harbor area, rode past rowhouses, and saw the street hustle in action. I was in the car with a stranger, but for some reason, I already knew I would attempt to pursue some type of situation-ship with him. This night would become more than just a thrilling joyride. It would lead me down a path to a travesty lifestyle that I never thought I would travel in a million years. When I woke up the next morning in my dorm room, I could only put together bits and pieces of the night before due to the alcohol usage. My roommate Dev usually went back home on the weekends, so I was there alone. I had no clue what college life would look like besides what I saw on the TV shows I watched on BET and the commercials I saw. I didn't have a mentor or anyone to tell me what to expect, the dos and don'ts or "stay away from this and that." I believed I had to totally figure out how to navigate life on my own and live in this world. This thinking process of stubborn and strong independence was deeply embedded, though. It was a result of learning to make my own decisions, whether good or bad, in my youth as a latchkey kid.

At the age of nine, I somehow became partially responsible for another human being, a little brother seven years younger than me. He had a nanny, but it was my job to get him there before school and pick him up afterwards. My mom worked to make ends meet and kept a roof over our heads. I salute her undoubtedly for that. So, during my adolescent years, until I left for college, I was figuratively my brother's second mother—making the decisions, calling the shots, and telling him what he could and couldn't do when Mom was at work; making sure he ate dinner and went to bed on time. I never asked for this level of responsibility. It became my rites of passage for being a part of the family. And this responsibility spilled over into my own life: not only did I assist with the decision-making for my little brother, I also made personal decisions for myself without the direction and consultation of my (at the time) workaholic parents. Hence, my decision to go to a school I had never researched and getting myself involved with a drug dealer—a person who most certainly did not have my best interests at heart and who used me for his selfish ambitions and personal gain with my full consent.

After my initial spontaneous night with Shawn, we continued to kick it. He lived about 10 minutes away from campus in a shabby rooming house with a disgusting shared bathroom used by other men that always required shoes upon entering. With no car at the time, pickup and drop-off times happened out of convenience and during creeping hours. Sometimes, I would come back to the dorm just in time to take a shower and get ready for my afternoon class. I reeked of marijuana constantly because I had connections to an insurmountable supply.

I barely made it through my first semester academically. When I received my first semester's transcript with my grade point average, it was humiliating, a whomping in the face: 1.0. This embarrassing GPA had nothing to do with my learning capabilities per se; it was a reflection of the time, attendance, and efforts I had failed to put into my studies. I was captivated by the lies, lusts, deceits, and distorted views of an unwholesome man.

Awkwardly enough, there were no movie dates, going out to eat, shopping, or anything else true couples or friends did. Instead, like a cycle, I went from my dorm to his place, to riding around Baltimore, back to his place, and back to my dorm. Any talks about boundaries or commitment were not established. Quality time was nonexistent. I basically assumed and came to my own conclusion that we'd become something more, rather than what I truly knew deep within. I tried to spend as much time as possible with him. I thought I wanted to be his one and only in my young, adulterated mind. But no matter the efforts, it just wasn't happening, to say the least. What's more, I became the girl who could be trusted with the stash, supplies, rides out of town, and late-night creeps.

Over the course of three years, I learned more about street life than about how to be a successful college student or write in APA format. I recognized the difference between a Glock and a gauge, an ounce versus a pound, and how to be cunning. Plus, I couldn't stop thinking about whether someone was going to try to rob me or even kill me for my associations. Shawn would tell me crazy and gripping stories about the hustling life in Baltimore City. Someone was always getting robbed, stabbed, shot, or imprisoned. It was like an eye for an eye, tooth for a tooth principle. And one of the known rules was to never give out your real name or share with anyone in the game where you really lived. If anyone did, they were liable to get hurt out of greed, jealousy, and revenge.

SPRING '04

At the school I attended, there were two girls who didn't care much for me, and they made it known anytime we interacted and shared the same spaces. I was oblivious at first to their hostility toward me, until I found out from friends or Shawn himself what the real deal was. Nika was from New York, and she peeped how close Shawn and I had gotten. Supposedly, she and Shawn were just really good friends, but I strongly believed it was more at one time or another. Nika started hanging around my small circle on campus a lot more than usual. Even though Shawn and I were just kicking it, I had my eyes on another guy named Tion. When Nika found out, she told Tion in front of my face. His reaction was a rejective and embarrassing one. She laughed and also told Shawn about it. Any kind of butterflies I had before were certainly now gone.

One night, I was chilling in my dorm room, and I got a call from the room phone saying that someone wanted to meet with me. She wanted to talk with me about something, but not over the phone. I was given the room number, and I told her I'd be up soon. I let my roommate Gabrielle know where I was headed and that I'd be back down shortly. I couldn't help but think this had something to do with Shawn. Oh, I was right. Here I was being confronted about messing around with him. She asked me if I knew he had a girlfriend and all these other weird crazy chick questions. I kept my answers short and to the point. In my mind I was thinking, "Who the heck is she? Where did she come from? She not even cute! Why is he talking to her? How did she find out about me?" So many thoughts ran through my mind that evening. Thankfully enough, our conversation was pretty civil. There was no fussing, fighting, or carrying on. However, at the end of the conversation, no agreeance was made. We only knew of each other.

After the conversation ended, I headed back downstairs to my dorm room in a fury. I had never been approached by another woman about a man. I immediately called Shawn to get things straight—no answer. I pounded my fist harshly on the dresser near a box of hair clips; a few moments later, I noticed my hand was bleeding. Deep down inside, I wanted to be done with this guy—and for a little while, I tried to, in my own strength. That night, I didn't hear back from Shawn. He called a day or two later, only to tell me when I confronted him that Zain was lying and she wasn't his girlfriend. Oddly, I believed him. Shawn claimed no one as his girlfriend.

Zain probably felt the same way I did about Shawn. More than likely, she had hoped to be with him long term and maybe even after college. Did she know he was a drug dealer, though? I mean, Zain was super smart, participated in numerous school clubs, was liked by her peers, had an academic plan, and had much more going for herself, as I gleaned over time. But who knows, maybe she was doing all the things any normal girlfriend would do, yet he wasn't committed. She may have even thought she could change him. I know I did.

SPRING '05

When I moved into my apartment off of Loch Raven Blvd., it was less than a 10-minute drive to get over to Shawn's. I once saw Zain coming out of his apartment. At least a year had passed since our first interaction. From snooping around Shawn's apartment, I found out that his place and cell phone were in her name. He couldn't sign a lease in his name due to an extensive criminal background over three pages long. From my perspective, this was the game he played—prowling on young, impressionable women to get what he wanted at any cost. There were so many telltale signs indicating that I should run, run away from this life and never look back. I slighted the internal nudges from Holy Spirit to seek help because I was unaware of His voice. I thought it was my subconscious talking. No one knew about the lifestyle I was living, not even my close friends. I hid this part of my life until it ruptured. The ride was wild, very reckless, and ultimately shakable.

Chapter 2

Let the Fight Begin

**The vast majority of incarcerated females
have experienced abuse in their lives
("Words from Prison").**

WINTER OF '92

I hated going over to Sharon's house. It was a place where
the adults partied consuming bottles of alcohol, smoked
cigarettes, and played loud house music, and all the children
had to go downstairs to the basement, outside, or out of sight.
In my direct household, there was no drinking, smoking, or
loud parties. Sharon's house was the spot for all the family
to get together regularly and have a so-called good time.
Oftentimes, I would be one of the last people to leave, because
my mom usually stayed to help clean up. The basement was
fully decked out with a TV, sofa, game table, full bar set, and
musical equipment. When I was still in my toddler years, this

9

was the place where my two older cousins and I would gather to sing and play music. I was the lead singer, Derrick played the drums, and Alan played the guitar. Sharon's longtime boyfriend Huey let us use his equipment and usually video-recorded us having a ball. It was a fun experience. I enjoyed music and had a true passion for singing. Singing would carry me through the dark times ahead. My aunt would always encourage me to sing at family gatherings, as she saw the gift operating in me early. Unfortunately, this was the only fond memory I had of being at Sharon's house.

Sharon had two sons, Derrick and P. Derrick was the oldest. He was five years older than me, a trickster and mean-spirited. One night in the basement, Derrick asked me if I wanted to play a game. I asked him what game, and he said Doctor. At first, he was referring to the kids' game Operation, which is "a battery-operated game of physical skill that tests players' eye-hand coordination and fine motor skills" ("*Operation* (game)"). It started off as a pretty fun and innocent game. Then, Derrick made a comment that we should play Doctor on each other. I had no idea what he meant or what he was implying, but I followed along. I was seven years old, and Derrick was a young tween. His brother P remained glued to the television the whole time. We went around the back of the couch. Derrick took the lead. His version of the Doctor game was one of perversity and no boundaries. Derrick thought it was okay to touch me in places I had never been touched before, and he required me to do the same to him. At seven years old, I had no desire for sexual stimulation. I was a bookworm and a school nerd. Those acts didn't feel right. I didn't know if this was normal. Was this what cousins did to play together? I felt fear and immediate contempt. He was older and bigger than me, a beloved member of the family. Playing the Doctor game in Sharon's basement happened more than once. Derrick took every opportunity he could to violate my space and young body unjustifiably. Whenever he said "Let's play Doctor in the basement," I knew what he really meant.

To add to that, I had another cousin who was around the same age as Derrick. I'm not sure if the two of them were close, but they certainly grew up together. Our moms were close-knit sisters, so we were constantly around each other. My aunt saw me as her own, and my mom vice versa. Therefore, it was normal for my cousin to come over and spend the night at our house. Sometimes, we shared the same bed. I had been staying in what was really a family room, but when my uncle moved out to get his own apartment, I got his old room. My new room was at the back of the house across from the kitchen where my mom made delicious, mouth-watering meals. Finally, I could close my door and get my first glimpse at privacy. My own personal little space with a window. The space where I sang, danced, and recorded Aaliyah songs from the radio on a blank tape. I had a Cabbage Patch Doll, Sabrina, who I held closely at night. When I wasn't doing homework, I would go over to the neighbor's house to play outdoor games like Double Dutch, tag, or hide and seek. Since my brother was only a baby, I often played by myself with Barbie dolls. Those childhood moments were peaceful and stress-free.

When Alan came over, though, he was a nuisance. He was always getting into trouble, causing a ruckus at his house. I know my aunt loved him in her own way, but Alan felt more connected to my mom than to his own. I was completely content spending time alone in my room. I had plenty to do: fix Sabrina's hair, listen to music, read, solve puzzles, bake goodies in my Easy-Bake Oven, or watch TV. Alan was uninvited. He was an only child, so maybe he wanted a little sister or something. I don't know. I just knew I didn't want to be around him. He was too fixated on me. Too playful and very competitive when it came to getting my mom's attention.

I don't exactly remember the specific details of when it actually started, but I remember the space where it took place multiple times: my room. My sacred space of solitude. The place where I could be myself, enjoy my own company, and fantasize about my future. This space became a vivid nightmare after Alan entered it. Alan molested me several times. I could see the sickening excitement in his eyes as he would show and tell me what to do in the dark. It looked fun and pleasurable for him. However, I only felt more disgusting with each act. There wasn't enough soap and water I could use to wash away the filthiness I felt. My self-worth became tarnished. I was shattered, filled with self-hatred, numbness, abandonment, rejection, bitterness, and unforgiveness. When I looked in the mirror, I saw nothing good nor innocent. I only saw anguish and ugliness.

Somehow, I still managed to do well academically in elementary school. I repeatedly got listed on the A & B Honor Roll and received awards up until fifth grade. Yet, emotionally and socially, I was a wreck. I cried more often and barely spoke up for myself. I only really talked to Shanytah and Ebony, my elementary school best friends.

FALL OF '93

Being teased by my peers only made matters worse. I was picked on for my height, having large lips, and getting hair underneath my arms at eight years old. I took every offensive word personally and tucked it away in my hippocampus for later use in my self-destructive thinking habits. Back then, I thought I did my best to suppress my anger, until a situation triggered an outburst. In my third-grade class, there were a few students who would roast me regularly. This day in particular, I was ready for war. I was tired of being picked on, and I had witnessed enough fights at school and in my hood to know what to do. One of the girls kept picking on me, and before I knew it, I had grabbed her shoulders and body slammed her on the table while the teacher was out of the room. When the teacher came back, that same group of students tattle-told on me, and I was banned from going on the school's trip. I was glad I stood up for myself that day—not in the manner I chose, but after that, no one in that class bothered me.

The molestation continued. For a while, it felt like a normal part of my life, because I didn't know anything different. Were my cousins in cahoots to destroy my life? Did they plan this? Was this their way of picking on me? If so, it was a horrible way. When other family members were around, Derrick acted like I didn't exist, and Alan couldn't control himself from teasing me or being annoying in some manner. He even went as far as inviting himself on a summer vacation to my dad's house, an invitation I didn't approve of. My mom and dad never married, and my dad resided in the Jersey Shore area. Summer vacations were usually a blast—a time to escape, have a sense of peace, enjoy the beach, and ride my bike all over town. My mom let me take my bike with me. It was a mountain bike, turquoise and purple, the prettiest bike I had ever seen.

Since Alan had come with me to my dad's that summer, I guess he thought I was going to hang out with him or show him around. Wrong. I wanted no dealings with him. I already knew my way around, and I knew many of my dad's associates. One day, coming out of the church my dad attended, I went to get on my bike, and Alan got the urge to take it. I tried to take it back from him, but I fell to the ground and bruised my right shoulder, which left a scar. I couldn't stand this boy. I couldn't understand why he was like this, and he thought it was funny. I told my dad what he did, hoping Alan would get put on the next train back to his mom's house. But he only fussed him out, gave him a lecture, and demanded that he give me back my bike.

My dad was a part of Set Free Ministries, a radical ministry that preached the gospel of Jesus Christ via street outreach all over. The home base was in California, but this sector's church was located in Asbury Park, New Jersey, on the corner of 5ᵗʰ Ave. and Memorial Drive in the same shopping plaza as a popular West Indian restaurant where we got bangin' Jamaican beef patties for a dollar. Set Free Ministries was the place where I heard a compelling and genuine message about Jesus Christ when I was still in my youth. Somehow, I understood what the speaker was saying and instantly believed in my heart and confessed with my mouth that Jesus Christ, the Son of God, died, was buried, and rose again for someone like me. Once that confession was made, I didn't necessarily sense any sort of drastic change in myself, but I believed Jesus Christ existed and felt His presence.

WINTER OF '95

Some time later, I found out we were moving to another city in New Jersey. My mom told us it was a place with better schools and neighborhoods. She didn't want my brother and me to grow up around street violence and be subjected to drug and gang activities. I had mixed feelings about the move. On one hand, I was sad to be leaving my childhood friends and teacher, but on the other, I was glad that my cousins would be farther away from me and I would no longer be subjected to their traumatic behaviors. I hoped to bury the mess that happened to me so I could move on and enjoy a peaceable childhood with what was left of it.

We moved to a small, unknown suburban township in a three-bedroom condominium. The area was nice and quiet, a family-oriented neighborhood with access to a park, basketball court, and pool. I was in the fifth grade. This new school was a real adjustment because there were only two other students in my class who looked like me and the academic workload was way more challenging than my previous school. It was all so foreign to me. I certainly felt out of place and misunderstood on my first day of class. The other students sounded so polite and upright. They spent months staring at me and trying to figure me out, while I basically stayed to myself and barely said two words. My fifth-grade teacher at my new school was a great storyteller. She had a beautifully designed treehouse in her classroom where she'd invite us to lounge or sit on comfy bean bags while she read classic books to us like *Roll of Thunder, Hear My Cry* and *Let the Circle Be Unbroken*. She had our little minds depicting every character and line read. She was the only teacher I ever came across in this school district who expressed sincere interest in teaching students about diversity.

I struggled to catch up academically upon entering this new school. I was alienated from a desire to learn due to culture shock and no longer being the smartest person in the class. I was jealous of my peers for their advanced intellects and for having supportive parents who showed up to school functions and took strong interest in their studies. I felt alone and disturbed on so many levels, and I was struggling to deal with my insecurities and pains appropriately.

In the meantime, I found an outlet to escape my troubles. There was an elementary school nearby that hosted community indoor activities on Sunday afternoons. I got the scoop from some neighborhood kids who went regularly and decided to go. It was a cool place to be. We got to play sports and do arts and crafts. Plus, they always fed us pizza. One of the guys who oversaw the events recommended I participate in sports. My mom got the information and signed me up for intramural sports, specifically a community basketball team for kids in my age group. It was fun. Since I was taller than most kids my age, I played center or forward positions. My ability to make shots wasn't all that great, but I understood the functionalities and goal of the game. Sometimes, I would go to the basketball court by the pool to play one-on-one, HORSE, and twenty-one, or three-on-three with the boys. I was considered a tomboy since I played rough.

FALL OF '96

Other relatives lived in our neighborhood as well. We all lived on the same street, with our condo as a geographical middle point. My brother's grandmother lived by the pool, and his aunt on the opposite end. My mom worked a lot. We spent a significant amount of time with them playing games, eating, talking, and watching movies. On Sundays and Bible study nights, we rode in a family van to a Pentecostal church. I remember one day my girl cousin (on my brother's side) and I were at church playing around. The pastor had given an altar call about receiving Holy Spirit. Back then, I had no idea what that even meant. As we were joking around, I told her I was going up to the altar to see what would happen, if anything. I overheard people speaking in tongues and worshipping God. Prior to this moment, in the mirror at home, I had attempted several times to repeat "Hallelujah" over and over again, just to see if I could speak in tongues, as I wanted to test the myth I'd often heard.

When I went to the altar, I lifted my hands and repeated the prayer orchestrated by the pastor. Next thing I knew, I was moving my feet and speaking foreign words I had never spoken before. My mouth was moving uncontrollably. Then, I knew I had received the baptism of the Holy Spirit. After the indwelling, I headed back to my seat, and my girl cousin smiled at me as if to say, "I told you, Donna, not to play with God." She and I got along so well. We could relate to one another. We shed many tears together throughout our younger days and once planned to run away from home together. She was my cousin-sister-friend. Her boy relative was an imposter. On dark rides home from Bible study nights, he would tell me to sit in the back seat of the van so he could stick his hand up my shirt. Other times, he would tell lies to his mom so she would agree to let him leave the house to visit ours.

Did I have an invisible sign on my forehead or heart that read "weak girl here—come and find out," in which only boys who understood this telepathic communication would be put to the test? Ugh. It was awful. My brother's relative had a thing for me, and although we weren't biologically related, I still considered him my cousin and wanted him to leave me alone. He took pleasure in being able to caress my girl body parts, and the evidence showed up in his pants. This wild boy even tried to convince a few of his other cousins to pursue me. I did not ask for this. I did not want this perverse attention. I never flaunted and I never giggled. I was numb and untrained in how to speak up for myself. I had no courage to tell my mom what was going on.

The travesty of my self-worth ruptured. My outward sadness was a coverup for my anger beneath, and my anger was an ongoing mental pain until I dealt with it. Alan almost caught the aftermath of my anger the last time he attempted to take my bike and acted like a jerk in front of a group of friends. He kept taunting me, and I finally had enough, so I grabbed a knife and headed for the door when he ran out. My girl cousin's friend instinctively tried to take the knife from me, but I was on a mission to put this nuisance to an end. She and I tussled for a few seconds, which seemed like several minutes, until the knife twisted deep around my right index finger. Blood poured out, and the focus was now on getting me to the emergency room to get stitches. Someone called another relative to get me there because none of us had a driver's license yet. We made up a bogus story to tell my mom, since she was at work. It was a crazy and hazy afternoon. I had made my point to Alan, though. No more would he come for me. That escapade was a rap. There was a power shift. At the age of 11, I had an epiphany that child molestation was wrong.

Living in a new town was a very slight relief from my previous childhood woes. I went from surviving one battle only to endure the next. I wasn't mature or equipped enough to know the power of my voice. Although I had confessed Jesus Christ as Lord and received the baptism of the Holy Spirit, the journey I traveled to recognize and come unto a full understanding of my worth in God, which uncovered my true identity, would feel like hundreds of thousands of miles away.

Identity Crisis

Trauma can sometimes cause us to use our bodies to glorify our inner pangs.

SUMMER OF '99

Over time, I adjusted to living in a new town and attending a school where a majority of the people looked different from me. I found my own little tribe of friends, and we hung tight until our teenage years. By our freshman year of high school, a couple of them moved away or had a personality change that suggested we part ways to chart our own paths. For some of us, we jumped into the waters of dating and pursuing cute boys. It was a lot to process as hormones started shifting and sexual attractions arose toward the opposite sex. Blue and I made a secret bet to be accomplished by Christmas of 1999. Both of us kept our word and shared what we thought at the time to be fun, desirable outcomes. It made us wild, rebellious, and too experienced for our age. This secret bet was a catapult to a stressful, promiscuous teenage life.

I met my first boyfriend at Surfside Spuds, a food place at the mall where I worked part-time. He was two years older than me, chocolate and about 6'2". He lived in the city where I attended elementary school. Since this mall was the closest to his hometown, and NJ Transit offered a direct route to and from the mall, it wasn't out of the ordinary for him to be there. He was pretty easygoing. I introduced him to my mom, and he came over frequently. We listened to music and talked. I cried a few times, but he couldn't understand why. I wasn't willing to share with him the specific details of that vulnerability. Yet he may have come to his own conclusion about what happened to me. We were in my room chillin', and one thing led to another. I was dressed, sitting on top of him, moving my body in suggestive ways that caused him to question whether I was really a virgin or not. I stopped due to embarrassment, and he asked, "Donna, where did you learn that from?" I remained silent. The relationship only lasted for a short while. I wasn't looking for anything serious or long-term. Caring about his feelings or mine was insignificant. I believed if I could get his attention, then I could get the attention of another male, and this belief prompted me to give him the boot.

FALL OF '00

After some of my close friends moved away, I met an unpopular girl at school who lived in a group home. Aryt was a few years older than me. She sought after guys who were much older than her, and she appeared to thoroughly enjoy doing it. She used her curvy physical attributes to entice them, while using a soft baby voice to convince adult men to buy her what she wanted. Then, she would turn around and spaz out on anyone who got in her way. This was on another level for me. It was what most would call "the game"—a game of manipulation to get what you want. She had two main guys she kicked it with regularly, and then there were others who she smoked weed, drank with, and just had feel-good times with. Hanging out with her made me feel grown, like I was in control. I learned from her how to approach men, lie, and get their attention. I started hanging out in Newark, New Jersey, on a regular basis. Forget hanging out at the mall—I thought I was doing it big by rolling with her. She introduced me to Cubans and Puerto Ricans, gang members and money makers. All I had to do was engage in small talk, look cute, and never carry my ID. Yes, I was scared. It was the risk I took to feel accepted.

I got so caught up in hanging out with her that I skipped school and didn't come home for two days. By this time, Aryt had moved back to Newark and found her own apartment. She invited me over to chill, smoke, and drink with her peeps. I thought I was having a good time. I didn't call my mom or tell her where I was going. I planned to come back when I was good and ready—not taking into consideration the consequences or how worried my mom must've been. The details of how she found out where I was staying that day she came for me are a mystery. Najee, one of Aryt's boyfriends, came back to the apartment telling me a woman was at the corner store showing my picture and asking if anyone had seen me. I was nervous as all get out. Before I could get my belongings and flee, I heard my mom's voice from the bay window, hollering my name to come outside. She hollered multiple times before I got the nerve to move toward the door. When I came downstairs to meet her, I was greeted with a big slap across the face. She told me to get in the car and not EVER to do that again. My mom was terrified of the thoughts running through her mind concerning my two-day disappearance. She was scared to death for my safety. We drove back to our condo, and I never hung out with Aryt again. Thank God my mom rescued me from my own destruction that day.

When I came back home, I was supposedly grounded for some time. It didn't mean much, because my mom worked a lot and often during third shift. It was easy to stay up late, wait until my brother fell asleep to sneak out for a couple of hours, and return home before dawn—or bring the party to my house when I was home alone and clean up really good afterwards. I decided to hang out with a few different girls my age, two from high school and the other from work. I got a new job at an assisted living facility, working in the dining room. It was a fun, simple job, serving meals to the elderly residents while working with other teenagers and getting free meals to eat after shift. My new friends traveled to Newark with me to go shopping or meet someone off the chatline. The chatline was where people called in via telephone and stated their names and profiles to connect. Individuals could select who they wanted to speak with or decline. If both parties expressed interest, then they would exchange numbers to chat offline and potentially meet up. In my circle, no one ever went alone. We went out in pairs and came up with excuses when the environments looked odd or someone lied about how they looked over the phone. Looking back, I know it was nobody but God who spared my life and got me out of some icky, careless situations.

My teenage years were reckless and irresponsible for the most part. I perceived I was raising myself and tried to compress my feelings of loneliness, abandonment, rejection, and anger by living carelessly and neglecting my true worth. Being called names by family members devalued my identity. When I did something wrong or got in trouble, I was called a foul word or referred to as stupid. When I attended family gatherings, I was called a string bean, too skinny, and given the nickname "smut" without knowing what that word truly meant. I was picked on and called unpleasant names so many times I believed it. The saying "sticks and stones may break my bones, but words will never hurt me" is a lie. I got over the beatings and never experienced the broken bones, but the maleficent words spoken stung deep to my core, broke me down, and dwindled my God-given identity.

To make matters worse, I had a wedged relationship with my dad. He came back into my life when I was eight years old. I received a letter from him telling me how much he loved me, missed me, and wanted to be present in my life moving forward. When I first wrote back, it was out of fear and anger. My words were filled with bitterness and sorrow. I was still mad that he had left in the first place. He was the one who taught me how to brush my teeth. He would take me out for car rides around the city in his blue 1970 Mustang. It was cool to hang out with him. Then, all of a sudden, he was gone for a while.

The letter explained his absence. He gave his sincere apologies and spoke about his life experiences and newfound transformation. After having a conversation with my mom, I eventually came around and decided I wanted him to be a part of my life again. Everything was going well. We were getting to know each other. He would come pick me up on the weekends and during the entire summer. We once traveled on a three-day group road trip across the country to California. I rode on the handlebars of his bike when he didn't have a car, and we used to go to the basketball courts and Pizza Plus in Asbury Park regularly.

Somehow, all that time we spent together started to decrease. I was growing into a teenager, and my dad had gotten married for the first time. It all happened so fast. I was still able to go to his house on the weekends and summer breaks; I just saw my dad less and spent more time with my favorite cousin. As soon as I would touch down to my dad's house, either he was asking me if I wanted to go over my favorite cousin's place or I was requesting to. My dad worked endlessly. He had a full plate, and spending time with me seem to fall to the bottom of the list. I was the black sheep of his new family. His wife had three children, and she made sure that my dad always looked out for them first and foremost. I would get the casual leftovers, which included a meal, a movie, or helping out with a task. And she almost always had to come with us when we went anywhere. Even when he came to pick me up or drop me off at my mom's house, she rode with us. There was no privacy to discuss anything.

I get that my dad was maybe trying to get us to bond. However, I had another thought in my mind, that maybe she was controlling him. Most of the time, whatever his wife said was the final way of how it was going to be. I often bumped heads with her. She hollered and yelled, and I did not like seeing her disrespect my dad. Things were so jacked up that I couldn't even have a key to get in the house—a house that I came to at least three weekends out of the month and for summer breaks, and where I participated in cooking and cleaning duties. To get in, I had to wait until someone arrived or call beforehand. It was crazy. And my dad did nothing to change it. So, going to my favorite cousin's apartment was a no-brainer. It was somewhere I would feel accepted with no tension. We played pranks on people, got on WebTV, ate Chinese food, hung out at the mall, and traveled to New York together. We genuinely loved and looked out for each other. When I wasn't at my dad's house for the weekend, my favorite cousin and I would still link up on the weekends and talk on the phone weekly. He was one of the few people I confided in concerning my relationship with my dad and the new family dynamics. He shared his feelings and insights on the matter too.

I remained hopeful that the relationship between my dad and me would get better. It bothered me so much. I never had the guts to tell him how I truly felt. From my perspective, he was the adult, and I was the child. I longed for his advice and care. I wanted him to tell me I was beautiful and show me I was truly loved. The more he kept pushing me off to go to my favorite cousin's place, the more I felt rejected and unprotected. I navigated New York as a teenager, rode the subway trains, and attended nightclubs with little supervision besides my older cousin. I questioned if my dad cared about me, because his check-in calls came in only rarely. I thought he cared about his wife, her children, and his money more than me. And I wished his actions would have proven me wrong. As a teenager, I had no belongings in my possession, nor on my back or feet, ever given to me by him. We never had conversations about boys, sex, money, or other life skills. He did come to one of my basketball games with his family. We laughed after the game because I tried to chase down on the court one of the girls on the other team who knocked my glasses off while I had possession of the ball. Although we had moments of laughter together, our relationship was distant and in need of repair.

SUMMER '01

At some point, my dad's wife and I started to casually get along. I matured in my conversations with her, and I visited much less. I was spending more time on the weekends with my party friends and going places I had no business being. Sometimes, I ended up going to Plainfield with my mom and brother to visit Sharon mom's house for a family event. I would say hello, grab my plate, and after I finished eating, head outside to avoid my former perpetrators. I couldn't bear to look at them and be reminded of my guilt and shame. Alan tried to make small talk and act like we were tight. I only felt sorry for his limited physical condition. Before he reached age 18, he was in a bad car accident that left him with a spinal injury and no movement in his feet. When I first heard the news of his new physical state of being, I was saddened and remorseful. For goodness sake, he was my relative. But then I thought to myself, "This is his punishment for what he did to me."

Internally, I was feeling a little arrogant and conceited when I went to family gatherings as a teenager. In secret, I was getting the attention of young adult men in their early 20s. I attempted to dress and act older than I really was. A promiscuous lifestyle had the noses of teenage boys and men wide open for me. They could smell my stench of perversity. While I used my cute looks and youthful body to entice them, I glorified my body in an attempt to suffocate my inner pangs. No amount of sexual activities could fulfill me. I was searching for wholeness from the trauma I experienced early on.

Besides that, most of the male role models in my family were involved in the criminal justice system. Some of them were in and out of the joint continually, serving years upon years at one time. It was nothing for one of my male cousins to serve a 5-7 year sentence only to turn around and do another 10 years. They had more certifications and degrees in street hustle than college degrees. I was dragged along on visits to a men's facility, not by personal choice, on multiple occasions before the age of 14. I witnessed supposedly grown men treating women I loved like scum.

To add to that, high school had become boring, and I was doing the bare minimum just to get by. Regularly, I attended in-school suspensions and skipped most Saturday detentions. Sadly, the assistant principal knew me by name. The mental turmoil I suffered from gave me no breaks. I remember sitting in my walk-in closet in the dark on numerous occasions, weeping and wailing about my life, or singing worship songs in the half-bath near the kitchen with the ventilation fan running loudly. Singing and reading books were ways to escape my reality. I wanted to change my life, but I didn't know where to start or what to do. This would not be some kind of easy fix or attempt to go cold turkey. Looking back, this journey involved battling spiritual warfare, breaking generational curses, denouncing dysfunctional family lines, seeking counseling, and so much more.

By senior year, I was practically coasting in my academics. Somehow, I managed to pass all my tests and classes to be eligible for graduation. I had three classes in the morning, and in the afternoon, I went to my co-op at an elementary school, acting as a teacher's assistant in a math class. The students were a joy to be around, as was the teacher. I graded papers and participated in group activities. On my last day, they surprised me with a mini fridge as a going off to college present—a sweet gesture and unforgettable moment.

My mom threw me a graduation party, inviting relatives from both sides of the family. When Dwayne arrived, I told my parents I would be back in a little bit. I was just going to the end of the driveway to say hello and get my graduation gift. Dwayne and I had started dating in my junior year and had been steady since. Mom knew we were dating, but Dad knew nothing about him. My dad came outside on the porch and said, "Baby girl, what are you doing? Come back inside. You got all these people in here." I said, "Okay, Dad," and tried to finish up my conversation with Dwayne. My dad looked irritated, called my name a few more times, and waited until I came back up the stairs. He tried to give me a mini lecture about having Dwayne come to my graduation party and explained how rude I was for going outside. What he said went in one ear and out the other. I was thinking, "How dare you say anything to me about being rude or not entertaining guests? You barely know anything about me—or Dwayne, for that matter." Dwayne was actually supportive and protective of me. I had a quote-unquote "real boyfriend," and one who treated me fairly good. He did not appear to be with me for any kind of selfish gain, and I was headed off to college in a couple of short months. Dwayne held no qualms about my dad's outburst and went home that day.

SPRING '03

Heading off to college was exciting. I wanted to get out of New Jersey and see what it was like to live in another state. I hoped Dwayne and I could continue with our relationship, since Maryland was only three hours away, but he declined. He said he couldn't bear the thought that I might meet someone else of interest while away at college. He was all too familiar with college life, as he often visited his best friend at Hampton University. His truthfulness sounded reasonable, and I willingly accepted our fate. Who knew I would meet someone who would potentially turn my world upside down?

Chapter 4

Out of Bounds

**My poor choices were tied to childhood
traumatic experiences.**

SUMMER '03

My last summer in New Jersey as a teenager. I was headed
off to college in late August. Originally, I imagined attending
the University of Tennessee and getting a shot to play with
the Lady Volunteers. The coach was phenomenal, and one of
my favorite players from the late '90s went to the WNBA from
the squad. My wishful hopes were a fantasy. The reality was,
I wasn't going to play for any basketball team, and my GPA
was only good enough for a college that accepted basically all
applicants. I was headed to Maryland with no real plan—no
money and no major. It was a good thing to be encouraged
to attend college by peers; however, there were no mentors
in my life who I could seek for guidance. Some saw college

as an escape route from the streets or a path to live a better financial future. I had a desire to go—to become someone new, to have a career, and to make money. When I reached out to some family members for any kind of financial support to attend college, there was a hefty dismissal. Even a few bucks would've helped me out with something.

Therefore, I tried to figure it out on my own. I went, explored, and I crumbled the first time around. This was my first time away from home for a long period of time—and out of state, for that matter. Making new friends, managing classes, living out of state, and learning how to become an adult was overwhelming. All my past traumas were still haunting me. Even away at school, I managed to attract guys who saw the invisible mark on my forehead that read "trauma-affected, proceed in ambush." The cycle continued. For the longest time, I couldn't figure out why this kept happening to me, or why I allowed myself to get into regrettable situations and behaviors, then withdraw and not allow others to get close to me. A dysfunctional pattern. The enduring effects of multiple adverse childhood experiences were prevalent in my life.

I read that adverse childhood experiences (also known as ACEs) are potentially traumatic events that occur during the first 18 years of life. "ACEs can include neglect; physical, emotional and sexual abuse; household challenges of parental separation, substance misuse, incarceration, violence and mental illness; and social factors such as economic hardship, homelessness and discrimination" (Bradford). By the time

I was eight years old, I had already gone through multiple traumatic events that included witnessing domestic violence, experiencing molestation, and the separation of a parent. According to statistics, almost one in nine children nationally has experienced three or more ACEs before reaching the age of 18. "Nationally, 61% of black non-Hispanic children have experienced at least one ACE ... compared with 40% of white non-Hispanic children." In most regions, the prevalence of ACEs is highest among black non-Hispanic children (Sacks and Murphey). Trauma related to single or multiple events experienced by an individual "has lasting adverse effects on the individual's physical, social, emotional, and/or spiritual well-being" (qtd. in "What's Your Concept of Trauma"?). Each person deals with trauma differently.

As I've reflected over my life, I believe this to be true. My traumatic childhood experiences had long-term effects on my physical, social and emotional well-being. I found myself conversing with very few people. I was super quiet at home, and it wasn't easy for me to spark up a conversation with a stranger. I liked spending too many hours alone and refused to let others get close to me because of fear, abandonment, or future rejection. I was stubborn and cold to classmates' feelings and disrespectful to some of my teachers and friends. I tried to be tough when I really wasn't and kept a stone-cold face to look mean and unapproachable. I cursed random people out and expressed severe road rage. I disregarded love for myself and others. I was selfish and sneaky. Someone looking from the outside in would've probably labeled me a hot mess.

I took all my insecurities, doubts, fears, emotional suffering, low self-esteem, and other baggage with me to college. Up until this point, there was no one I felt I could confide in. My worldview was tainted. But the one thing I hoped to do was make my parents proud by becoming a first-generation college graduate. I expected to obtain my degree in 2007, land a good-paying job, and live independently. I'd hoped to figure out a way to fund my tuition and become an adult. It all sounded fantastic and achievable from a distant view.

FALL '03

When I arrived in Baltimore, I was ecstatic to be there. I was among other students who identified with my culture and aspired to become working professionals. There were so many organizations, clubs, and circles one could join. Some days, I hung out with the track and field team, and other times, I partied with the students who smoked marijuana. At summer orientation, I met a girl who asked me if I smoked, referring to marijuana. That's all she and I really ever did together. No studying, no shopping, nothing really productive. Whenever one of us broke college students found the supply connect, we would scramble up our money together and make one or two blunts to share.

After my freshman year, I got leery of smoking weed. I started having these weird hallucinations that I was getting ready to die, and I had something like an out-of-body experience that freaked me out too many times. Also, I was thinking about joining the military so I could receive 100% college tuition. My loans were adding up after just one year, and I didn't want them to tell me my total loan repayment of massive debt after four years if I continued with this method, so the free college tuition advertisement from the military was appealing to me. I met a recruiter who had a table set up outside the food court at Monmouth Mall. I worked at that mall, so I saw him regularly. After numerous approaches, I was persuaded to join. Paid tuition, GI Bill benefits, two professions simultaneously—yes, sign me up! My parents weren't too thrilled when I told them I was going to the military, but they supported my decision. This was only three years after 9/11, so getting called to go to Iraq was a realistic concern. The recruiter I spoke with promised I would be able to get into my field of choice as a dental assistant, yet he tried to convince me to become an 88M (meaning Motor Transport Operator)—or in civilian lingo, a CDL truck driver—one of the top most dangerous positions to accept and most needed during war. Needless to say, my plan for going that route backfired. I was back at square one trying to come up with a financial plan. I decided to work and go to school.

FALL '04

Throughout this timeframe, I was involved with Shawn kind of off and on. For about four months, I had no interactions or dealings with him. We spoke on the phone every now and then, and I wrote letters occasionally. I considered myself a player and wanted to get back at him for finding out about Zain. He didn't care. He loved the street life. His focus was on getting rich quick and receiving street fame.

SPRING '05

I decided to move off campus with another girl from my college suite. Everyone thought we were sisters because of similar physical features: tall, slim, full lips, football-shaped eyes, high cheekbones, and flat feet. We got along pretty well and shared personal stories. Both of us expressed dreams of modeling. After the fall semester of our sophomore year, we found a two-bedroom apartment to rent, and we paid the security deposit and signed the lease. Now I was geographically close to Shawn, but when he found out I had moved permanently to Baltimore, he expressed no real interest. In my mind, I was determined to get his attention, to get closer to him, to earn his trust and even his love. He was in love once before with a woman from the military, but she left him and their child, which left him with an emotional unattended wound.

I started hanging out with Shawn more often. I tried to gain QT (quality time) in the day as well as at night. Most times, he drove around the city making drops and picking up money. At some point, the demand got bigger for more than just marijuana. Bartenders, escorts, gang members, bus drivers, and whoever else were purchasing marijuana, pills, coke, and whatever else was sold. Shawn had the nerve to ask me once if I wanted to try cocaine. Adamantly, I declined. I was well aware of the many dangers in taking just one hit. That was a risk I was not willing to take.

Living with Ife became a real struggle. She laid on the couch for hours watching TV and delayed cleaning up in the kitchen for days after making traditional African meals. The bathroom held hair in the sink and the tub was filthy. She stopped paying her half of the rent and communicated much less. Everything had started out fine when we first moved in together, but there was an unknown mental shift along the way. I pulled my share of the weight with household chores and then some. I grew up in a household where living in filth was unacceptable. Certain areas had to be clean—the kitchen and the bathroom were no exception. Thus, I carried those same principles and practices while living with Ife.

The lack of cleaning was one thing, but when she stopped paying her rent with no communication, that was a whole other beast to deal with. I made sure to have my half of the rent every month, even at the expense of putting a halt to school and working two part-time jobs. Her behavior bugged me, and I got tired of paying her half of the rent. Being naïve,

I decided to move out without telling Ife or the apartment leasing office. I found my own place about eight minutes away. I met with a leasing agent, viewed the apartment, and signed the paperwork within a week. I figured being able to afford $700/month would be no problem. I informed my parents I was changing locations and living solo. They endured my endless complaints about Ife not paying her portion of the rent and what I personally considered disgusting living conditions. With haste, I made a feasible decision that would have a future negative financial impact.

SPRING '06

Shawn came over to my new apartment regularly. I had a washer and dryer inside my place, which was a win for both of us, I guess. He brought his laundry over sometimes to wash his clothes. He also had a silly idea to treat my apartment as his storage unit. I peeked into the green big duffel bag he left in the closet. There was enough money in there for more than a 20% down payment on a home, along with street supplies and weaponry. This was a sign he had started to trust me. I never touched any of the money in the duffel bag. I could easily have skipped town, moved and sold all the products and guns, but I wasn't that shady. I wanted to show him how loyal I could be so I could become his main chick. Yet it was a waste of time trying to please Shawn. He never committed, and the more loyal and trusting I became, the more useful I was to him as a resource. There was nothing in it for me. I was being used, and I felt every bit of it.

Once in a while, Shawn would give me a couple hundred dollars for the minor work I was doing. He was making more money within a few days then I made in one year. If I could get him to pay my rent regularly, I wouldn't have to work, or I could work when I felt like it. That's what I was thinking too, by the way. I was connected to a couple of temp agencies, so I held a few temp jobs here and there. I got a pink slip from the gym because someone reported I was sleeping on the job, and I just up and quit without notice at the before and after childcare school. I found another job that had pretty flexible hours, conducting store inventory audits. It was fun, and the people I worked with were hilarious. In between, on my days off, I was accompanying Shawn on road trips to New York and Georgia. I started taking half an ecstasy pill to stay awake at night. Everything I touched was felty, and grinding my teeth was normal. I got lazy and stopped showing up for work. I wanted to make more money and have Shawn take care of me. For all I knew and put up with, I deserved it.

A few times, I got behind on my rent and Shawn bailed me out. I kept crying "woe is me" to God every time I got a notice on the door, begging HIM on my knees to receive a financial blessing. The solution was there all along—keep a job, get on a budget, and pay your bills—but I wasn't trying to do that. I kind of went into a depressed state after I had a real shot at a job opportunity through a temp agency. It was a temp to hire position, making $10/hour, Monday through Friday, operating the switchboard via the Social Services Department. The stipulation was that I had to stay on as a temp for one year, and after that, I could get a dollar increase and gain a position as an economic eligibility caseworker. Not even a month went by before I was unassigned. A rep from the temp agency told me not to report back because someone notified them that I had used my cellphone while at my desk. Back then, there was a strong no tolerance policy for using a cellphone on the job. I placed the exact event when it occurred. My friend Nichelle had called my Nextel phone, and I answered because I thought it was an emergency. As soon as I told Nichelle I was at work, a lady walked in the office and saw me putting the phone down. There went that opportunity.

I was falling apart. The rejection stung from being fired from the gym and then being unassigned from a job that could have jumpstarted my career. My relationship with Shawn was heading nowhere. I was neglecting myself and my family. Sometimes I made trips up north and bypassed my parents' exits. Straight there and straight back was the focus. My friend Nichelle and I started hanging out more often. She saw the spiritual and physical condition I was in, and she attempted to steer me in the right direction and encourage me. Nichelle invited me to her church and introduced me to her pastor, who was her spiritual father and advisor. I went out to eat with them a couple of times, and I enjoyed the atmosphere. It was welcoming, peaceful, and accepting. Deep inside, I could feel the nudge to connect with them and seek help for my life. I started going back to church, attending weekly Bible study and Sunday services.

During intercessory prayer, I prayed for a way of escape to leave Shawn alone and take a different path. I desired to live a better, safer, healthy, and wholesome life with God. I wanted to live for HIM, follow HIS ways. I just didn't know how. Every time I thought about telling Shawn I was done, fear paralyzed me and held me in captivity. I was afraid of what he might say or do. I was in too deep.

I spoke with Nichelle's pastor several times. He would call me almost weekly to check in and see how I was doing. No funny business. He genuinely cared about me and offered to counsel me. I shared with him some of my past and the disoriented relationship I had with my dad. He provided some wisdom on how to handle a few situations and suggested what I needed to do to overcome. Nichelle's pastor became a confidant to me. I kept a notebook and wrote poems, and he listened to my poems and told me how good they were. I felt safe talking with him. I recognize how the Lord put him in my path as a way of escape, as an outlet for me to escape the ultimate trap waiting for me and go down a different path. The Lord was calling me, and I chose not to answer even though I had cried out many times. I think I was looking for something more miraculous from God, a more mind-blowing, cold-turkey experience rather than the vessel He put in front of me. This overlooking can happen to anyone.

I tried my best to make an intentional effort to stop contacting Shawn so much. But sometimes, when I didn't hear from him for a day or two, I kept calling his phone, leaving messages saying how worried I was that I hadn't heard from him. That was a waste of time because he never urgently contacted me back. He would call when he was ready to come over or to get something out of the closet. I continued my telephone counseling sessions with Nichelle's pastor, and Nichelle and I also spoke regularly. She supported my new endeavors to get a car, enroll back in school, get a job, and do something fruitful with my life. I considered joining the church, learning sign language, and becoming a part of the choir. I did join the church, but I didn't feel right getting involved in ministry when I was still fornicating and participating in other ungodly behaviors. It's not that I wanted to wait to join until I was perfect; I wanted to be consciously attempting to please God in my lifestyle, and I wasn't there yet. There was still a lot of mental and emotional turmoil happening on the inside of me. With the help of Nichelle's pastor, I was beginning to work through it unknowingly. However, the internal war continued, and I was unprepared and uninstructed on how to use my spiritual weapons to ward off the external fiery darts.

The last time Shawn came over my apartment, it sent a smoke signal leading to my breaking point. He dropped off his dirty clothes and expected me to wash them. This was the first and last time I washed his clothes. As I was going through his pockets, I found condoms and phone numbers. I was furious, and all kind of scenarios came across my mind. It's not that I was surprised by his behavior. I couldn't help but think about who he could be possibly sleeping with. Was it someone else I knew? Was it right before he came over to my place? I saw the image of the time when Shawn tried to holler at another girl in front of my presence, not even discreetly. Was it her? Were they messing around? My mind was spinning. Enough was enough. I was fed up with him, and I wanted to get him back. I wanted to get him back for all the time and work I put into this destructive relationship without ever getting a good return.

FALL '06

I wanted to forget about Shawn, and the only way I knew how to replace him was by seeing someone else instead of dealing with my total mess, so I decided to reconnect with an old flame. My neighbor helped me get a job interview with his company, and I enrolled in an online university to get a business administration degree with the help of Nichelle. Plus, I was being requested for local modeling gigs, which brought a spark to my life. Everything appeared to be going well until nearly one month after my 21st birthday. Shawn contacted me and tried to be all lovey-dovey, as they call it. He proposed that I make a drop by myself to Georgia. When he said Georgia, I thought, "Hmm, maybe I can go see my old flame and make some money to pay my rent." Ultimately, I was only hurting myself with this stinking thinking. After we discussed all the details and the plans of the agreement, the date was set. I scheduled a car rental in Shawn's name to make a one-day turnaround trip from Maryland to Georgia and back to Maryland, 10 hours each way. Since I had no ties with the connect, Shawn was getting picked up at the airport to meet him. I was simply the transporter. Later, I informed my ex-boyfriend I was coming to Smyrna for a quick visit because I would briefly be in the area for business.

Something didn't feel right the day I was getting ready to go make the drop. I was a little hesitant and had a queasy feeling in my gut. I've had similar feelings since in other circumstances, but now I know it's Holy Spirit warning me with caution. I ignored those warning signs that day—I never considered the possibility that I might not make it back home. I packed a small bag, retwisted my locs, got a pedicure, put a couple of ecstasy pills in my purse, grabbed my two phones, and went to pick up the rental car. Shawn gave me specific instructions on what to do. He made it clear that I was to go straight there and come straight back.

The drive down wasn't too bad. The traffic was minimal until I got into Atlanta. I picked Shawn up from the airport, and he drove to the spot. The place was in a nice suburban neighborhood and had cameras all along the home. Multiple cars were parked in the driveway. Shawn went inside for about 10-15 minutes, then came out with $20,000 worth of pills. We headed to the airport for Shawn to catch a flight back home. He was hoping to see me within the next 10-12 hours. After I dropped him off at the airport, I headed to the restaurant to meet my ex-boyfriend. We ate, talked, and then went back to his dad's apartment. I planned to stay for only a couple of hours and then get back on the road. His dad, a military vet, must've sensed something odd going on, because he kept asking why I was in town and how long

I would be staying for. He offered to let me spend the night, and I accepted. I checked on the product in the trunk to make sure everything was intact. Shawn kept calling my phone to see where I was. I lied and told him I was on the road making a pit stop because I was tired. He kept calling for hours after that, and I stopped answering the phone. I thought I was having a good time reconnecting with an old flame.

I got up super early the next morning and checked my phone to see I had over 10 missed calls from Shawn. I should have been home by now, according to our plan. He was more concerned about the product investment than about my safety. I told my ex-boyfriend I had to head back and that I would see him another time. I got in the car and headed for the gas station. It was going to be a long ride, and I decided not to take the e-pills I had in my purse because I had never driven under its influence before and didn't want to take any chances, so I went inside the convenience store and grabbed a six-pack of Monster energy drinks.

As I was pulling out of the gas station, I noticed a cop car at one of the pumps. I didn't think much of it, but I should have taken it as a precautionary sign. I headed for Highway 85 North to get back to Maryland. Shawn called again, and I answered this time. He knew I'd spent the night with someone else but wanted to make sure I was on the way with his package. I estimated the time of arrival, got off the phone, blasted the radio, and cruised toward I-85 North.

Traveling back was a struggle. I was tired. I made it to North Carolina without any pit stops, but then I needed to stop to use the restroom I watched for the next road sign with the rest area symbol on it. When I noticed it, I veered off toward the exit. I parked, turned the engine off, and got out of the car. I noticed a State Trooper car in the cut. I took a glance, and anxiety and fear washed over me. I hurriedly walked into the women's restroom. While in there, I tried to contact Shawn to see what I should do. No answer. He was working at his day job as a city bus driver. I thought about flushing the pills down the toilet or hiding them underneath the toilet to come back and pick them up later. I was panicking. Maybe the State Trooper sensed it from nearly 1,000 feet away.

I got back in the car after several minutes and headed toward the highway. The State Trooper had his car facing southbound as I was heading northbound. I was driving a red 2006 Dodge Stratus, which easily attracted the State Trooper's attention. He swiftly turned his car around as I was passing by and got on the highway. I tried to smoothly get an increasingly large lead away from him, but I could see in the rearview mirror that he was coming for me. I saw the flashing lights and pulled off to the right shoulder. He stepped out of his vehicle. When he came up to the driver side of the rented vehicle, I pressed the button to roll down the window. He was a tall (about 6 foot), older Caucasian man, probably in his early 50s. He asked me if I knew why he was pulling me over. I said no. He stated I had made an unsafe lane change movement. The State Trooper then proceeded to ask me questions like "Do you know this area is well known for trafficking drugs? Do you do drugs?" and other drug-related questions. He asked me where I was headed to and where I was coming from.

Ultimately, he was trying to figure out if I was traveling with drugs, and he did. The trooper asked if he could search my car and kept me there for several minutes. I responded yes as I was ignorant about my rights and the law. He asked me to get out of the car and into his vehicle. Next, another State Trooper pulled up to the scene with a search dog. The German Shepherd searched the entire vehicle. The dog first sniffed out my two pills inside my purse, which the State Trooper held up for me to see. Then, the dog paid close attention to a specific location in the trunk, where the pills were buried, not perceptible by sight. The search dog barked, indicating he had found something. The State Troopers went over to inquire, and there was the stash. One of the troopers rewarded the dog for his findings.

I stayed in the trooper's vehicle. Someone else was coming to inspect the car further for any other drugs. I overheard one of them mention something about draining the gas tank. I was in shock. I was watching my own movie or *Cops* TV show happening right before my eyes. The State Trooper was saying something to me, but I drowned out every word. He took me to a nearby FBI station. I remember seeing signs for Winston-Salem and then Davidson County.

The State Trooper left me in the hands of the FBI. There were about five to seven men in the room, wearing their blue jackets with yellow FBI lettering. I sat in the chair, still in shock. All of the FBI agents drilled me with questions for about an hour: "Who did you do this for? Who's your connect? Give me a name. Give me a person." I refused. I wasn't going to talk. I was less afraid of the FBI's interrogations than of the repercussions I could face from the other people involved if I told. I didn't want to be labeled as a snitch or put my family in harm's way. I'm not sure if it would have been that severe, but I couldn't take any chances.

After the FBI finished drilling me, two local county officers came to pick me up. They handcuffed and shackled me. I attempted to walk down the steps, and my ankles hurt from the pressure of the shackles. Reality came over me like a stormy rain cloud. I was on my way to jail for the first time ever. The weight of humiliation and embarrassment rested heavy on me. I arrived at Davidson County Jail, an entirely unfamiliar place to me. As I was getting out of the cop car, one of the officers said to me, "You're going away for a very long time." I looked at him like a deer in headlights, hoping he would be so wrong.

We entered the jail processing center, where they took my picture and recorded my fingerprints. I went into a holding cell and was given a cordless phone to make a phone call. I called Shawn to tell him where I ended up. He was surprised and couldn't believe it. He promised to bail me out and be in touch soon. He scurried off the phone to avoid a trace.

That was the only call I was allowed to make. After a couple of hours in the holding cell, I went into the changing area and exchanged my civilian clothes for an orange-and-white striped uniform. I gave up my purse, jewelry, and any other personal belongings. The $179 I had in my wallet was put on my books for commissary. I was escorted upstairs to B block. Not knowing what to expect, I hardened my facial countenance before entering the block. The women had just finished up chow time. I sat on the bench peering into the eyes and souls of the women behind the bars. They stared back, probably wondering what I was in for. I had no idea when I would be going home, but I knew I would be spending the night in Davidson County Jail for the first time on a thin, green, hard, cold mat with no pillow. Dang, had all my adverse childhood experiences really led me to this?

Chapter 5

Woman UP

The storms in our lives tend to reveal our greatest strengths.

That day, October 2, 2006, flipped my entire world upside down. I was arrested and caged in a treacherous jail block among women I had never met before from all walks of life. I sat on the bottom bunk trying to figure out a plan to get out. I hoped Shawn was coming to bail me out as soon as possible. I looked around at where I had ended up and immediately realized this wasn't a place I wanted to become accustomed to. It was moldy and raunchy. A place with no wind, sunlight, or blue skies. There was no yard time to enjoy the weather, bottled water to drink, or delicious meals to eat. It was an atmosphere filled with strife, mischief, sadness, grief, loneliness, brokenness, and despair. A place of unrest and darkness. That night on the bunk where I lay down after lights out, a rush of fear swelled up inside of me over the thought of not returning home and being stuck in jail until only God knew when. I turned my face toward the wall and cried silently so none of the women could hear me.

The next day, I got up at 6 a.m. An officer unlocked the steel door to the block and the cells we were in to serve us breakfast. She called each woman by her last name to pick up a brown food tray. When she called my name, I went to the door, received my tray, and looked at the food in disgust. There was no desire to eat. One woman asked me for my tray since it was untouched. I slid it over to her and watched her eat it as if it were the best meal she had ever received.

The jail officer let us stay out of our cells for several hours after breakfast. We could take a shower, play cards, cell hop, or use the phone. I darted to the phone multiple times to make as many calls as I could to let someone else besides Shawn know where I had landed and to request help. The magistrate set my bond at half a million dollars, claiming I was a flight risk even though I had no prior arrests and the current charge was considered nonviolent. Since I only had about two to five minutes for each call, I said hello and got to the point quickly. I gave my name, location, and address just in case I would never to get to speak with them again based on the phone restrictions and whether the person could receive or accept collect calls. The first week, I called Shawn, my parents, my favorite cousin, my neighbor, Nichelle and her pastor, and my ex-boyfriend. I was able to get a hold of all of them, thankfully. It was a lot for them all to take in. There were so many questions they wanted to ask me, but time was limited. My plan was to try to get them to raise money for my bail. $50,000 was a lot of money to ask for, but certainly doable if attempted. No one was going to put a lien on their home in exchange for my release to a bail bondsman. It was a serious risk. After getting in touch with all the numbers I remembered by heart, all I could do was wait.

In the meantime, I kept quiet. I didn't tell anyone about my charges or share any information about where I was from. I read books by Danielle Steel and went without showering for days because I didn't plan to stay long and the shower area should've been condemned. I was assigned a public defender until my family could hire a paid attorney. When we initially met, he told me I was facing a total of 28 years for three different charges: manufacturing to sell and deliver, possession, and drug trafficking. The state of North Carolina follows a strict schedule chart that determines mandatory sentencing in cases like mine. Therefore, my public defender suggested I write down all the names of individuals involved in order to lower my forthcoming sentence. He also expressed that the district attorney's office knew I wasn't capable of doing something of this magnitude on my own based on my nonexistent criminal history and character. Without me saying a word, he shared how unfortunate it was for many women to commit drug trafficking crimes on behalf of their male partners. When he mentioned this, I had no idea of the statistics, but over the next several months in jail, I would hear of similar stories.

After speaking with the first public defender, I communicated the news to my family. I knew nothing about the judicial system or what rights I had from the jail cell. My dad helped me to navigate the entire process. Shawn and my mom had been communicating back and forth on my behalf. He mentioned that if I could get my bond down to $75,000, then he would be able to bail me out. I asked the public defender, and he stated he would speak to the judge. My first request was denied, so it would be several months before the public defender could try again.

By this time, the red nail polish was chipping off my toenails. I wasn't allowed to have nail polish remover or razors, so the hairs on my legs were getting long. My locs hadn't been retwisted in months. I bought several items from the commissary to help me along the way, like writing pads, pencils, envelopes, stamps, white underwear, socks and t-shirts and shorts, Lady Speed Stick deodorant, and snacks galore to substitute for the meals. When I finally made a courageous decision to use the shower, all I had to dry myself off with was half a towel. I made sure to bring my t-shirt and undergarments with me to the shower so I could put them on before exiting. Although the shower area was really gross, I'm glad it was only available for one person at a time with some privacy. It was one of the closest activities to the normalcy of the outside world.

While at Davidson County Jail, I switched my cell to stay in another with Shauna and other women. Shauna spoke to me freely like I was a family member or one of her homegirls.

She gave me the tip to read books in order to pass the time. It worked for a little while, as long as it let my mind drift into fantasy to keep from thinking about everything on the outside such as Shawn's whereabouts, my apartment, school, family/friends, modeling gigs, and everything else I'd taken for granted.

Shauna gave me her spiel concerning what she was in the joint for, and I got comfortable enough to share too. We had similar stories, and we bonded like sisters close in age as she awaited a final court date. She had been in the county jail for nearly a year. Her court date kept getting rolled over for continuation, and there was nothing she could do about it. She was a North Carolina native with a bright, angelic smile that lit up our cell and the spirits of anyone who saw it. She was always positive, full of laughter, and hopeful. Shauna became my role model for such a difficult period in my life. She encouraged me as long as she was in B block and told me I would be able to get through. Eventually Shauna was shipped to the Department of Correction (DOC) to complete the remainder of her sentence. She took a plea deal for three years, with almost one year down already, and was as happy as can be to go to prison so she could at least work instead of lying around in a jail cell passing the time away. I was sad the day she left, but she assured me I would be all right. She promised to write to stay in touch. I was grateful our paths crossed. Prior to meeting her, I had not experienced such kindness of a stranger, despite the conditions in which we met and considering my standoffish personality due to previous traumatic experiences. I went on to meet more women over the next year or so who helped my waiting game become bearable.

SPRING '07

Keisha came into the jail after Shauna left. She admitted to having a gambling problem that led her to incarceration. This wasn't her first rodeo in jail. She knew the process. She had a husband who could bail her out if he wanted to and children to take care of at home. Keisha's husband wanted to teach her a lesson and help break her bad gambling habit. She confided in me about her struggles and loving her family dearly. I attempted to encourage Keisha amid my own challenges. She had a deep tenor voice and a bellowing laugh. We played cards together and shared stories. Keisha didn't take any mess from anyone on B block. With her booming voice, she cut down with words those who tried to disrespect her and never apologized. When she left, it was bittersweet. I was happy to see her go home to her family but disarrayed from losing the friendship we had built.

Filled with anxiety from thinking about the outcome of my situation and from other stressors, I had thoughts of committing suicide. There was no way I could spend 28 years of my life in prison and be okay. Suicide seemed like an easy solution. I thought about stealing a whole bunch of medication and shoving it all down my throat. Many of the women received medication for a variety of ailments and disorders. It would be an easy bribery to pay them with commissary in exchange for their medications. Typically, they would have to take their medication directly in front of the nurse, but many of them became skillful at fake-swallowing the medications to save for later or give to someone else.

I held on to my suicidal thoughts until one Monday night when Ms. Gail, Candace, and the other three church ladies came in. We were separated by bars, but they came in vociferously singing, clapping, stomping, giving praises unto God, and encouraging us to hold on. They sang hymns and popular gospel songs, welcoming us to sing along. I sat on the bench holding on to the bars as their voices offered refreshment to my burdened soul. I was desperate for any sign of relief, and I was awestruck and amazed by their encouragement. They had one hour to fellowship with us. Ms. Gail asked me if I was new here, and Candace asked if she could pray with me. I responded to them both, saying yes and telling them how I'd never been in jail before and was hundreds of miles from home. I was given a Bible, and Candace recommended I start with the book of John. She prayed for me in her soft, tender, motherly voice. She told me she had a young daughter who she loved dearly. As the time drew near for them to leave, she held my hand and told me she would keep me in her prayers. I thanked her. I held on to the Gideon Bible given to me. I anticipated the next Monday, and the 50+ more after that, for their weekly return as a beacon of hope.

I started reading the Bible, beginning in the book of John just like Candace recommended. It was a fascinating book that spoke about Jesus Christ being the Savior of the world, and how He came to redeem and give us eternal life. One scripture in particular struck a chord in me when I read it: *"So, if the Son sets you free, you will be free indeed"* (John 8:36). The words "free indeed" stood out mostly because that's what I desired: to be free from emotional and mental distress, the jaded and awful memories of childhood trauma. To be forgiven by God, to be free of my past, and to be free of any feelings left for Shawn. To be truly free indeed. If Jesus Christ could make me free from all this, then the freedom was a guarantee. So, plainly speaking, if I decided to surrender my former life and behaviors, confess my sins, and turn toward God and follow Him, then according to what I was reading, I would have that freedom. And that promise was enough for me. I thought to myself, "What do I have to lose? I've tried so many things before, so why not give this a try?" I made a conscious decision to believe the scriptures and, even from a jail cell, put into practice what I was reading.

The next time I saw Candace, I shared with her what I had been reading in the book of John and the revelations I had received. She smiled and encouraged me to keep reading. She also briefly shared her own personal testimony with me. I was shocked and awed at what God had done in her life. I decided to keep reading the Bible because I wanted to see what other promises, declarations, and directions were in it. I developed a hunger and thirst for the Word of God. I wrote down scriptures on my notepad, tried to memorize as many as I could, and highlighted key scriptures that stood out to me while in my storm. When I was ready, I made a public confession and rededication in front of witnesses (the Monday night church ladies) of my serious commitment to God. I confessed out of my mouth and believed in my heart that Christ had died and risen again for me. This time was different from when I was only a child. Somehow, I understood the full magnitude of Christ's birth, death, and resurrection and that He personally thought about me when He hung on the cross. And from that day forward, I made it my aim to build a relationship with Him. I noticed that I stopped reading romance novels and my speech was gradually changing.

One day while I was reading, lying on the bottom bunk in the cell, I noticed I had no anxious thoughts. I wasn't thinking about the outside or worrying about my life. The only way I can describe it is as if I were standing on a beach watching the waves, with no other sounds or cares in the world. I asked myself, "What is this?" and then it hit: PEACE. I was experiencing the peace of God for the first time in my whole life. My mind became a testament of the scriptures about peace. It was so refreshing. The eyes of my understanding were being enlightened, meaning I was able to digest the basic principles of the Word and apply them even while I was in jail. I began writing and singing songs. Nay and I co-wrote a few songs together and ministered them in front of the other women and the Monday night church ladies. I held small, intimate Bible study groups, and God laid it on my heart to pray with and for the women on a nightly basis. We held our own revivals. Some of the women were even released from jail miraculously. Building my relationship with God became my coping method to endure this hardship.

SUMMER '07

The next time I met with my lawyer, he mentioned that the DA was willing to drop my plea deal down to 14 years. I still wasn't satisfied with that offer and was unwilling to accept such a horrible plea. My mom reached out to an attorney, giving him $2,000 in advance to take on my case, but we never heard anything from him after he received the money. I kept in touch with Shawn whenever possible. He sent me a few letters keeping me up to date with what was happening on the streets. He said people on the streets were giving me props for holding it down in jail and not snitching, basically. I also received praises from some family members who were all too familiar with this lifestyle. We called it street credit. If I held out and completed my bid, I would have a street credit degree versus a college degree. Whatever praises they were giving me, I could care less, because I had already made up my mind that I would never go down this path again. I was more concerned with witnessing to Shawn and others about accepting Jesus Christ in their lives and telling them about the inner transformation I was experiencing.

Mostly, I kept in touch with my immediate family and support group through writing letters. I wrote about seven or eight pages per person to get out everything I wanted to share in one sitting. Oftentimes, I ended up encouraging them unexpectedly. Nichelle and I kept in touch the whole

17 months I stayed in jail. She always kept me posted about her latest life updates while sincerely asking how I was doing. She wrote in a letter that she drove all the way from Maryland to North Carolina by herself to visit me, only to be turned away because she wasn't on the visitation list. It saddened me to learn how geographically close she was to seeing me, only to be denied. I appreciated her willingness, love, and support towards me. When I inquired about the visitation list, I made sure to add her and a few other people just in case. The letters, books, cards, and money I received from family members and others meant so much to me. I surprisingly received letters from a couple of Nichelle's church family members who didn't know me. It was a blessing and a constant reminder of how valuable my life was and that I mattered.

I continued to encourage other women in B block as much as I could. But the closer I drew to God, building a relationship by reading the Word and living it out, the more I had to deal with the oppression and temptations from the devil. I started having demonic nightmares and perversive images come to my mind. It freaked me out so much because these were events I never even dared to think about or imagine. I wondered if I was going to lose my mind. I became so anxious that I started pulling my locs out unintentionally. I couldn't control the images in my mind, and the images would make me feel paralyzed for hours as I focused on them so much. I never actually lived out those temptations or images, but it was very challenging to endure and resist.

In the season I experienced this, there were very few people I could confide in about it because I didn't think most of them would understand. I happened to share this with another woman named Toya who was in the jail at the time. She told me her mom had experienced something similar and she would get her to write me. It was a little comforting knowing someone else had experienced this before. Toya's mom wrote me and explained that I was going through spiritual warfare. She gave me some suggestions to combat those lies and deceptions by declaring the Word of God and pleading the blood of Jesus over me. This spiritual warfare I experienced reminded me of the time the Bible speaks of in Matthew chapter 4 when Jesus was tempted in the wilderness by the devil. I only wanted to have the peace of God on my mind instead of experiencing spiritual warfare. I knew nothing about spiritual warfare, and I'd never heard any pastor I had encountered ever explain it. I got through it by the grace of God and with the help of Toya and her mom. The supernatural fight between good and evil was real.

Toya and I became really cool. She told me she was a hot mess and wanted better for herself and her eight kids. She wasn't afraid to get in fights, and she was well known around town for doing so. She called herself a beast and praised her fists. She had a lot of brothers, so fighting was the norm. Standing at 4'11", Toya cried like a baby when she got emotional talking about her kids. She sucked her thumb and tucked her hand under one of her breasts for comfort when walking around the Block. I enjoyed talking to Toya.

She kept it real. I found out Nay wanted to hook up with her, but Toya wasn't having that. She made it very clear she only desired men's body parts, and eight kids were the results. She threatened to knock out anyone, including Nay, who attempted to approach her offering sex.

At first, I didn't like Nay. I thought she was nasty for trying to convert women on the Block to desire her. I wanted no part of her tactics and stayed away from her as much as possible. Toya and Nay were still cool after Toya told her she didn't get down like that. I had never been exposed to an environment like this, and this was around the same time I experienced spiritual warfare. Over time, Nay and I at least became spade partners and wrote a few songs together. I grew to understand her and see her through the eyes of Christ.

I measured the time I had to spend in the County Jail based on the time of others who I connected and got along with. If she had four or eight months, I knew doing time would be endurable and I would get closer to an ultimate solution. I faced the reality that I would eventually go to prison. Some jailhouse lawyers thought I should get probation for five years, and others said I would do a mandatory sentence of three years. The jailhouse lawyers were the women who had been in and out of jail for years, learning what specific charges carried a certain amount of time. It bothered me so much as I would see so many of them come and go over the course of my time there. I thought, "Just give me a chance, and I'll be sure to never enter this territory again."

The lawyer who was originally working on my case sent me a letter letting me know he had moved to another state in the Midwest and I would be reassigned to someone else. I wasn't upset, as he didn't do anything above or beyond on my behalf. My brother stole the remaining $4,000 Shawn gave my mom to hire a paid lawyer, so that was a wash. The next public defender assigned to my case was a woman. She was well known and labeled as a good public defender throughout the jail. At our first meeting, she gave me a rundown of what she would be presenting to the DA and how inclined they may be to agree. I left the visit feeling a bit more hopeful than previously, as her recommendations would be significantly less than serving 14 years and winding up with three charges on my record.

WINTER '08

A few months later, the woman lawyer came back to see me for a visit. She cut straight to the chase, telling me a plea deal had been offered for 70 months with only one charge. She suggested I take the deal, as this would more than likely be the best deal I could receive. I told her I wanted to consult with my family first and I'd get back to her. She told me I wouldn't have long to make a decision, and I agreed to get back with her in about a two-week timeframe. I headed back to the Block and straight to the pay phone. I contacted my dad and whispered to him all the details the woman lawyer provided me. I thought to myself that 70 months would be a long time to survive in a prison, but I was ready to move on from the County Jail, and I had made it this far. I had been there for 17 months. Some women ended up waiting even longer depending on the severity of the crime. My dad encouraged me to take the plea. I trusted his sound advice concerning this serious matter and agreed to it. I followed up with the woman lawyer and gave her my consent to the terms. She told me she would have me in court very soon.

Cautiously, I began asking a few women about prison life. I wanted to prepare myself mentally for what was to come and watch out for danger. Some of the common responses were that prison was way better than being in jail because the time goes by faster and there are options to work and/or go to school, complete activities, and stay busy. They shared that prison wasn't a happy, fun place, but it was manageable if I had survived this long in jail without medications, insanity, foul behaviors, and adapting to so many other jailhouse misconducts. Their responses brought me no comfort, though. Prison was a bad place, and having lived through it, I still hold the same position today.

After meeting with the woman lawyer, I started giving stuff away here and there since my court date would be arriving any day soon. It wasn't like I would get some kind of notification from an officer or receive an incoming call from the pay phone, so I just had to be ready. I let Lizeth and Nay know I would be leaving soon. Lizeth was originally from Mexico and spoke very little English. I tried to learn her language as much as I could so we could communicate back and forth. She was kindhearted and in a similar situation to me—the only difference being that she was pregnant with twins and couldn't receive the proper prenatal care she needed. Lizeth left for a short while during my waiting period to deliver her babies. She faced deportation, and I wasn't sure if I would see her again. When she came back to B block, I was surprised to see her. She was no longer pregnant. I could tell by Lizeth's expression that she was saddened to leave her babies with a stranger to go sit back in a jail cell. Before I left, Lizeth gave me two pictures of her twin baby girls. She chose one of her baby girls' middle names especially after me. It was an honor and a blessing for her to do such a thing. Because of it, we would never forget the impact we made on each other.

The day of March 3, 2008, came. It was another regular day on the Block. I was watching the newly installed TV through the bars mounted on the wall in the catwalk area. The catwalk area was where the jail officer conducted her rounds to either count us or make sure we were breathing, or where the church ladies stood when they came to visit us. I heard the steel door unlock. The jail officer opened the door and hollered my name, informing me it was time for court. I rolled out of the top bunk and stepped onto the steel sink, then the commode to get to the floor. I grabbed the gray bucket from underneath the bottom bunk to find my jail uniform. I put the shirt over my head, put my arms through, and pulled it down over my waist. I pulled up the matching orange-and-white striped pants and slipped into my white-colored black-bottom flip-flops with socks on. I took a quick look in the permanently smudge-stained mirror on the way out of the Block. This was the best I could do. I headed downstairs with the jail officer to the courtroom.

I stood next to my court-appointed attorney. We went through all the judicial dialectics and processes. I told the judge how I pleaded, and he explained to me what that meant. The judge ordered me a mandatory sentence of 5 years and 10 months for a drug trafficking charge, crediting me with all the time I spent in jail toward my sentence, and a $50,000 restitution fine. Therefore, I had about a little over 3 ½ years remaining. I walked out of the courtroom nervously relieved to be leaving the horrible county jail. On my way up back to the Block, I saw the bright sun glaring through the windows. This was the first time I'd seen the sun in over a year. On the Block, the windows were high up with bars fastened to them, keeping out the sunshine. My complexion had significantly lightened about three shades because of it.

Basically, I mentally checked out of the jail after court. I was ready to focus on the next part of my journey, which involved facing the fears of going to prison. The officer who escorted back to the Block had been there since my initial arrival. She must've sensed my anxieties, because she sure enough gave me a word of encouragement to calm my fears. I went to bed that night praying to God to give me the strength to persevere.

In the middle of the night, the jail officer called my name for DOC shipment. I was being transported to a maximum-security women's facility in North Carolina. I hugged Lizeth and said goodbye. I told Nay to keep her head up and hang in there. I grabbed all the items that were most valuable to me.

As I exited B block carrying my big plastic bag, I didn't look back to see what I might have left behind. Ms. Gail and one of the other church ladies had given me their addresses so I could keep in touch. I endured so much turmoil, witnessed many women go through drug use withdrawals, backed-up commodes, fussing and arguing, being on suicide watch in a turtle suit for seven days, and power trips from officers in Davidson County Jail. I wouldn't miss the physical place at all. However, the stories, prayers, and struggles of the women who were so much like me, I would always carry in my heart. This was the day to proceed forward with a new mindset and a renewed spirit. I had a true relationship with the Lord that I wanted to continue. I changed my clothes, hurried down the stairs, got on the bus, and headed for Raleigh.

6

Chapter

Getting Out of the Jungle

The courage to ask may open doors for you.

The ride to Raleigh was about an hour and 45 minutes. I couldn't sleep on the bus. I was wide awake. Although it was still dark, I enjoyed hearing the loud sound of the bus engine while staring through the window at the trees. It was around 3 a.m. when we finally arrived. We pulled up to a small, brown-brick, flat level building. Everyone on the bus waited for our next instructions before exiting. We were all handcuffed, responsible for carrying our own belongings. Once we entered the administrative building, we were no longer identified by our full name, but instead by a seven-digit number. If we had personal items we wanted to ship home, this was the opportunity. We couldn't have any items like our own personal bras, underwear, jewelry, or shoes.

The most humiliating part of the processing procedure was when a female prison officer called me into a secured area to take off my civilian clothes and ordered me to squat and cough three times. Embarrassingly, I did as she demanded. Standing in bare nakedness at 22 years old, I squatted down low enough for her approval, spread my buttocks apart, and coughed. This female stranger was looking directly at me, watching me complete such a horrendous act. It was a normal routine for her, as it was part of her job responsibilities to check for weapons and drugs upon entry of the facility. But it was a traumatic experience for me, and I'm sure it was for countless of other women who've ever entered a correctional facility.

After that, I was given a plain-colored stale dress to put on with brand-new prison panties and a white recycled polyester bra. All the women were then taken to the reception unit. It housed about 160 women divided into four pods labeled A through D. When I arrived at my assigned pod, I was given sheets and a blanket. I made up the assigned bunk, climbed up on it, and pulled out my Bible for comfort and reassurance. Generally, everyone new to the facility stayed on the reception unit for two weeks. We traveled in packs to the dining hall and were unallowed to communicate with general population. When those of us in the reception unit were outside on the grounds in a secured area, women from the general population would holler out "fresh meat" or make threats. It was a way to identify the weak, an attempt to scare us. I ignored every statement. I needed to maintain my focus and show no signs of weakness. It was a quick period to get adjusted to the new prison environment. My routine on the reception unit was to wake up, read the Bible, eat three meals a day, go outside for a bit, and write letters, though I waited until I got off the reception unit to contact any family members.

When my turn rolled around to leave reception, I was sent down the hill to Sparrow Unit first. Sparrow Unit was mainly for newbies or women who had any kind of drug-related charges. The judge who sentenced me also ordered that I complete some kind of drug treatment program and granted me the work release option toward the end of my sentence. I didn't have a drug use problem, so I was hoping not to have to complete a four-month D.A.R.T. program to engage in a treatment and recovery process. I hoped the long, boring assessment I took while on reception indicated I wouldn't be a good fit. Ultimately, I was able to bypass this requirement. I got called to report to Ms. Robeson's office. She was a case manager on Sparrow Unit with a military background. She never smiled, and she spoke harshly to everyone. Ms. Robeson reviewed my case notes, inquired about work experiences, and verified how much time I had. Once she realized how long my sentence was, she informed me I needed to work. She assigned me to the duplicating plant, a full-service print shop. She also gave me a written permission pass to the clothes house to get work clothes (shirts, pants, and work boots). Prior to that, my only option was to wear the ugly uniform dresses every day.

I stayed on Sparrow Unit until I was assigned at the duplicating plant. When I came back from work one day, the officer informed me I was moving to Phoenix Unit, better known as the Jungle. The Jungle was wild, loud, filled with all kinds of behaviors. I heard numerous stories and prayed nothing indignant would happen to me. The worst place to be in the dorm of the Jungle was by the red exit door. This red door, typically used as an emergency door, was the spot to gamble, smoke cigarettes, get a lick, and indulge in all kinds of other impermissible activities. I only went down to the red door to complete janitorial duties when assigned. I had a top bunk close to the entrance, facing the bathroom at an angle from the dayroom.

The dorm room I lived in was always rambunctious. No common courtesies were extended to any woman. The littlest amount of privacy one could find was in the bathroom stall, with a short door without a lock that another woman could literally peek her head over and take a look if she wanted. The shower area was foul—eight high wall shower stalls without any shower curtains, layered with grimy tile floors. The peace of taking a shower alone became a distant memory. At least in the county jail, there was a shower curtain provided for a sense of privacy. Even officers had the right to come invade the shower areas to see who was in there or what might be going on. Any ounce of dignity went unnoticed, extremely unrecognizable by prison officers.

I wanted to get out of Phoenix Unit as soon as possible. I attempted to stay out of the dorm as much as I could. I worked at the duplicating plant Monday through Friday, eight hours a day, making 26 cents an hour (a little over $40 a month). It was a whole lot of money in the facility compared to most of the other compound jobs, trust me. As I worked, I found other activities that would keep me busy. Some activities I genuinely liked, one of them being the choir. I always had a passion for singing, and this was my chance to join. There were no tryouts; basically anybody could get involved. We had a piano, a non-classically-trained choir director, and printed lyrics or hymns to sing along. All of the choir members rolled deep. Probably about 40 women participated in the choir. We sang during special functions or occasions, held a yearly anniversary special, and received goodie bags when allowed. I enjoyed being a part of the choir. For one, it kept me out of the Jungle as much as possible, and most importantly, it allowed me to express public adoration and worship toward God while also developing leadership skills.

The choir also allowed me to build camaraderie with a few other ladies, in particular a young woman the same age as me, just a month apart, who was serving a life sentence. We hit it off really good because of our similarities—same age, soprano voices, and hard knock childhoods. I expressed to her how I wanted to get out of Phoenix Unit, and she recommended I submit a move request letter to the "up the hill" unit manager, as we called it. Up the hill was mainly for long-termers and individuals with severe, persistent mental health conditions. I liked the sound of her idea. That same evening, I wrote the unit manager a letter listing all the reasons why I would be eligible to live up the hill besides not having 10 years or more on my sentence. Just a few days later, I shared the good news with the choir members that I'd received a letter back from the unit manager approving my request. I was elated. After choir practice, I packed up my things from Phoenix Unit and moved to Dorm G.

Dorm G was pretty laid back. It certainly wasn't as rowdy as the previous dorm I had left. Some of the choir members lived in Dorm G, so it was a smooth transition getting acquainted. The great perk about living up the hill in Dorm G was that I shared a small room about the size of a long, narrow walk-in closet with only one other person. Each room had a southern yellow pine door attached to it with a top window and no lock. I stayed in the last room at the end of the hall near the red door. I had one tall, standing, light gray locker and one under the bottom bunk, a footlocker storage for the rest of my belongings. There was a window inside the room where I often looked out at the sky and barbed wire that separated the "up the hill" from "down the hill" units. There were three shower stalls available, along with a laundry room on each hall. Living in the Jungle, I had put my clothes in a netted bag with my information labeled on it once a week for someone else to wash and give back to me the following day. Now I was able to wash my own clothes and take a shower privately again because of the dingy shower curtain that was hung up. Dorm G was not a royal palace; it was still prison. There was still an officer making rounds and taunting us, or someone fighting over something like another woman, canteen items, a card game, the TV, or just plain ongoing drama happening.

My bunkmate and I had the same last name and sang on the choir together. A tenor, she worked at the Travel and Tourism Call Center. Sometimes, she worked six days a week, which worked in my favor as it meant I had the room to myself. I spent a lot of time sitting on the top bunk reading, writing, studying, and reflecting. I had nothing but time on my hands. Staying busy made the time go by faster. Besides working at the duplicating plant and participating in choir, I attended weekly Bible studies and Sunday services sponsored by outside volunteers, and I enrolled in numerous continuing education courses. Plus, I visited the small library held in a classroom inside the academic building, checking out medieval, spiritual, and self-help books regularly. I continued to write longhand letters to loved ones and contact those who added funds to accept my collect calls.

The money I made at the duplicating plant was enough for me to get by on a weekly basis, except every now and then if I had to miss work because of the holiday or some other reason. I ate the food from the dining hall more than the food served in Davidson County Jail. Nothing super delicious, but it kept my stomach from growling. The meals I usually passed up were biscuits with sloppy gravy, molasses, and bologna sandwiches. Those foods were not allowed in my belly, nor the Red Delicious apples. It was something about the flavor of the apple skin that always made me feel nauseous afterwards. The times when I declined the dining hall, I chose to eat from the canteen. A canteen is like a store housed in one or more areas of a correctional facility that individuals have access to for purchases. The canteen was available at certain hours throughout the day. I purchased basic hygiene items, chips and sodas, Little Debbie cakes, rice, and ramen noodles (in Jersey, we called them "oodles and noodles"). Women were furious when the canteen closed unexpectedly or items were out of stock. They cursed at everyone in line, the officer on the yard, and the canteen worker. If someone asked another woman for a pack of oodles and noodles or a bag of chips, most of them charged at least double to pay them back. On a few desperate occasions, I asked someone to loan me a few items. Thankfully, she never charged me interest or asked for additional favors.

The prison grounds were pretty bare. There was no basketball court or volleyball net to play sports. It was filled with several oak trees, stone-age benches, and some picnic tables. Usually, some women sat near the infirmary feeding bread to the squirrels. The squirrels were so accustomed to the environment that they freely ate from human hands instead of running away. When I wasn't walking the grounds for exercise purposes, I could often be found having Bible study or conversing with another woman about her pain. I was no expert or therapist, but I had pretty decent listening skills, considering all the time I'd spent in the county jail hearing other women's stories. And I was intrigued. I admired the women I encountered in the prison. Some of them were strong, brave, intelligent, creative, and professional. Others were mothers, sisters, aunts, grandmothers, and daughters who got caught up or cried out for help, but no one listened or came to their rescue. Many of them had experienced childhood trauma, just like me. Prison was a pretty jacked up environment that only intensified previous traumatic experiences all while creating new ones.

Besides that, Shawn was still in the picture, though no longer at the forefront of my mind. I cared for him with the same hopes that he'd one day change, accept Christ, and see who I was becoming. The correspondence between the two of us via letters happened much less because he was doing time for another charge. And the street lifestyle, along with the women, held his attention way more than I ever could from where I was sitting. His mom stayed in touch, though. Every now and again, she was nice enough to accept my calls and hold a conversation with me for 10-15 minutes. She apologized for Shawn getting me into this mess. But I knew this was a result of the lifestyle I chose, and I was living out the consequences.

Neither Shawn, his mom, my family, nor anyone else could help me escape the predicament I was in. The prison culture could either break or make me, I chose the latter. Getting out of the Jungle (Phoenix Unit) and moving into Dorm G was the physical catalyst I used to dive deep within myself and seek God further. I occupied a small space of confinement to deal with the hidden and neglected issues of my past. I also met a few God-sent staff members who spoke life into me along the way.

Chapter 7

Seeking God, I Found Safety

Break the code of silence to release your heavy burdens.

The most valuable aspect of living in Dorm G was the time allotted to spend quiet time with God. Whenever my bunkmate was out of the room, I became very intentional about praying, reading/studying the scriptures, and worshipping God. I had a little clear-colored radio that took one AA battery, where I listened to on-air sermons from the outside world that always uplifted me. Vivi, the young woman just one month apart from me in age, was on the other hall too. We sang, talked, and prayed together frequently. She called me "little baby," a Southern term used to describe someone who looks way younger than her age.

Some days were really tougher than others. The feelings of loneliness and thoughts of regret would creep in to bring me down. Other times, talking on the phone with my family made those moods worse, but to prevent them from worrying at all, I never let them hear it in my voice. I cried numerous times in secret because I wanted to get out of prison. I was reminded every day of how I had relinquished that choice, and how badly I never wanted to return to such a horrible place. Vivi was an okay person to talk to, but I never told her anything real deep about me. She liked to focus a lot on herself. She could tell I was serious about living for God, though.

Since I was doing this on my own without any real spiritual counselors, mentors, or a pastor to shepherd me, it was a true learning curve. I developed a discipline and a level of commitment I never had before. I learned to maintain integrity in the presence of God and others, even when I felt like joining the crowd or giving up. This was another part no one told me years ago about becoming a new believer who is ambitious to take up her cross and follow Jesus: laying everything down to seek after Him takes *real* work. It's a battle. It's doing away with your old, filthy way of living and embracing a new way—God's way, as shown in His Word. I went to church on Sundays, weekly night Bible studies, and intercessory prayer meetings. Did I feel good afterwards? Yes. Did I leave changed? No. And it was no reflection on the teachings I heard or didn't hear. It wasn't the unanointed choir or because Ms. Cruella rolled her eyes at me. It was because my heart and my mind were not of one accord. They were sending two totally different messages to me. When my heart and mind linked up to the same beat, desiring truth, the lies began to dispel. For this reason, I became thirsty to know more about my true identity.

I sought counsel first from Holy Spirit because I knew He lived inside of me. If I followed the directions from the Bible, I would be just fine. These practices helped to change my mindset. I began seeing my place in the world differently, through a new pair of lenses. As my new lenses became clearer, there were questions I had and internal struggles I needed to face. The chaplains onsite were multifaith, believing in more than one religion. So, I continued to plow my way through my thoughts, questions, and internal battles independently. I read books by Derek Prince, Watchman Nee, Dr. Rebecca Brown, and many other spiritual authors. Their personal experiences with God were deep and rich, and the text was filled with wisdom. Turning over a new leaf was a daily process, a conscious deliberate decision.

Vivi always raved about an officer who was encouraging. Other women praised her too because they said she had a God-given ability to see and speak into the lives of everyone she came into contact with. I remember one day, some of the ladies from the choir told me they were headed to the tower to see her, asking me if I wanted to join. I was a little hesitant, but I said sure, wanting to see what all the hype was about.

We hurried over to the tower before count time. When we got there, I remained quiet, just observing. The other ladies made small talk with her, itching to see if she was going to say something revelatory concerning them. As I observed her during the conversation, I noticed the dimples in her cheek that illuminated her smile. She radiated with a glow I had never seen before. A voice soft yet strong enough to encourage one from a place of defeat to victory. She was a beacon of light to every woman on the compound. No one ever said anything negative about her or toward her. She was well respected and God-fearing. Everyone was always excited to see her. She never carried herself in a prideful way or raised her voice. She saw the good in others and treated us with dignity. From the day I met her until I transferred to a different facility a couple years later, she inadvertently became my spiritual mentor.

This God-appointed officer spoke to me in love with correction, edification, wisdom, and revelation. She challenged me to seek God more and more with a deeper yearning and commitment. She confirmed and reaffirmed what God had revealed to me privately. Often this God-appointed officer spoke of the unconditional, surpassingly untainted love of God toward me. She was a reflection of what a deep, intimate relationship with God really looked like. God knows she helped me significantly along my journey toward self-love. The wise counsel she offered led me to a place of surrender, to no longer wrestle against the truth of who God called me to be, how HE shaped me, designed me, and was using the time to refine me.

As I yielded to the refining process, I recognized the areas within that needed to be addressed. I could no longer carry all the weight and burdens of my childhood trauma.

The load was too heavy to bear alone. Nor could I continue to comply with feelings of guilt, rejection, bitterness, self-hatred, unbelief, and all the other stinky residue that came along with it.

The first time I told someone else about what I experienced as a child was in the arms of a caring woman of Pakistani descent, Abigail, who was serving time. She was part of the small circle of people I clicked with, and she happened to stay on the other hall of Dorm G near Vivi. Some of the officers on duty in our dorm were very lenient, which allowed us to visit whoever's room we wanted on the other hall. One night, Abigail and I were talking freely in her room about various topics. I listened closely as she shared her prior experiences concerning her former life and how she came to encounter the Lord. The conversation got deeper as we talked for well over an hour. Something in my gut moved me to blurt out softly with confession that I had been molested in my youth. I told her I didn't understand why it happened to me. She looked at me and held out her arms. We embraced for what felt like 30 minutes or more. Abigail rocked me in her arms like a mother nursing a newborn child until my tears ran dry. I felt the love of God hovering over me as if HE Himself was wrapping HIS arms around me, letting me know, "It's okay, daughter, I'm here for you. I've never left you, nor will I forsake you. You are MINE."

Close to 9 p.m., a sergeant announced over the intercom to prepare for count. I got up with all my snot rags and thanked Abigail for listening. My eyes felt swollen, but on my shoulders and in the pit of my stomach I felt lighter, refreshed from the presence of the Lord. I headed down the hall and around a few corners, landing on my bunk. I sat there thanking God in my mind as I waited to be counted by the prison officer.

Several days later, Abigail checked in with me to see how I was doing. I told her about the liberation I felt to finally tell someone my story. She smiled and nodded, then recommended that I go see Mrs. Kelsey. Abigail explained that Mrs. Kelsey could help me work through some additional struggles since she was a licensed mental health therapist and another God-fearing woman working at the facility. Mrs. Kelsey was located in Dorm E, a housing unit specifically for women with severe, persistent mental health conditions. This dorm was a restricted area. No one unassigned could enter without a pass or a call from the staff there. It was best to catch Mrs. Kelsey on the yard. She was a fast walker, so if we spotted her from afar, we would speed-walk to catch up with her.

When Abigail introduced me to Mrs. Kelsey, I was left in good hands. Mrs. Kelsey listened to the outpour moaning from my soul. She consistently prayed for me and walked alongside me throughout my healing journey. She radiated like the God-appointed officer. Unsurprisingly, Mrs. Kelsey and the God-appointed officer fellowshipped closely with one another. It was like an inhaled breath of fresh air having those two women on the compound who could pour hope into me. Whenever the God-appointed officer was on duty in Dorm G, she could always be found carrying on an intimate conversation with someone. Some of us posted up outside the office door to wait our turn for a word of encouragement. A few times, I found myself getting irritated when she wasn't available for discussion. The last time this feeling arose, I had to check myself because I did not want to get so heavily attached to her gifts that I couldn't recognize my own, or put God on the back burner when I could go directly to Him for every one of my emotional needs.

But I will say I believe the Lord allowed me to cross paths with these two women who helped me unveil the masks. They taught me to seek clarity and deliverance from the One who made me. Mrs. Kelsey showed me that beneath all the hurt, filth, shame, wounds, scars, and everything else in between, God was concerned about my tarnished condition. The God-appointed officer also reminded me that I was worthy of God's unconditional love. There was nothing I could ever do to stop God from loving me. All I had to do was recognize it, accept it, and embrace it—which meant I had to face the music, look in the mirror (so to speak), forgive myself and others, and dig deep within to pull up and root out all the baggage that didn't belong.

Chapter

Dealing with the Wounds

**Whenever you have the opportunity to
forgive someone, please do.**

The process to loving myself and knowing my worth in God was painful. It was gruesome, gut-wrenching, ugly, fretting, and yet so freeing. I spent days alone in my dorm room fasting and praying, asking God to show me the areas I struggled in. Sometimes, HE would reveal those areas in a conversation with another person, or through a dream, or by bringing back to my memory something from my youth in which the spoiled roots began. One area of struggle that always seemed to come up over and over again was rejection. I got offended so easily and held grudges as a defense mechanism. I took most things too personally when I should have let the words and actions of others roll off of me.

Dealing with rejection was out of my comfort zone because that meant I had to deal with the harboring feelings of bitterness against my dad. Internally, I criticized him and thought he could have done a better job as a parent. Through my lens, I saw him going harder for money and his significant other than he would for his children. Even though he never ceased to verbally tell me he loved me, his actions made it less than 100% believable.

I wanted him to do more, care more, and give more. I compared him to my mom unintentionally because she was busting her tail nearly every single night and day to provide for me. She never once complained or made excuses. I felt fury every time before my imprisonment that my dad said no—like the time I asked for a pair of sneakers for the new school year, or the time I inquired about getting help to pay for college tuition. Even $100 or a real explanation would have been better than nothing, especially after watching him give extravagant gifts to kids who weren't even his own. I was still hurting from all that, although this particular time in my life brought us closer together.

I asked God to show me the good in my dad, so I could stop looking at his failures and focus on what he was doing now. As the Lord dealt with me concerning this matter, I became more grateful to know my dad, to have him in my life, to learn more about him, and to embrace what support (whether emotional or financial) he did offer, like putting minutes on the phone to accept my calls, praying for me, and driving over 400 miles from New Jersey to a women's penitentiary in

North Carolina to lay eyes on his daughter to make sure she was okay. And there were other fond expressions of love in my youth from Dad that came back to my memory. It was a learned choice to love and accept my dad instead of wallowing in bitterness, thinking he rejected me when he truly had not. The more I understood and embraced God's love for me, the less I accepted this notion and spirit of rejection. I was NOT rejected. I was loved—loved by Father God and loved by the people who mattered most in my life.

More internal work needed to be done in me, and if I really believed God loved me and forgave me of all my wrongs, I had to come to grips with releasing unforgiveness toward others who hurt me and vice versa. The experience I had in Abigail's room was a critical step toward my inner healing. I wanted *all* my power back. I no longer wanted to walk around feeling downcast, burdened, and ashamed. With that, I decided to write everyone I could think of who was on my unforgiveness list, including my infamous cousins. Most of the people on the list, I knew their addresses by heart, so that wasn't a problem. The other addresses I needed, I got through another family member. I wrote for hours at a time on my 8.5" x 14" legal pad. My middle finger on my right hand had a big bump on the side from writing so much.

As I wrote the letters, I decided not to let fear take over me. The thought of what the recipients might feel or say crossed my mind. However, my true confessions were more important to me. In the letters, I spoke about my deep-rooted grudges toward the individuals and how they affected and negatively shaped my life. I mentioned the standalone moments in which their words had hit me like a super-fast, hard-pitched baseball bruising my head and leaving me with an untreated concussion for decades. It left my view dark and cloudy, preventing me from seeing the truth. Toward the end, I included a piece about how I forgave them, although I couldn't really tell by writing the letters whether I had or not. The real tests would come later. But it was an opportunity to start the process, to take action with faith and show God I was serious and willing to work through the pain to overcome.

The letters I wrote to the individuals I may have hurt were even harder. I mistreated people who didn't deserve it, because I was broken. It was painful to deal with knowing I had imposed some level of trauma on someone else. I hoped they would accept my sincere letters asking for forgiveness. Those I couldn't reach via letters, I prayed to God about. I prayed over all the letters I sent out, too, expecting nothing written back in return. It was another layer of release. I believed God would honor my efforts and do the work in my heart and mind toward a greater place of forgiveness.

The final letter in this litany of forgiveness letters was the one written to myself. It was just as crucial to write as all the previous ones. I held on to a lot of regrets and often thought about the opportunities I missed. I wasn't comfortable in my own skin. I had to come to terms with how I looked physically and accept all my flaws on the inside and out, how God shaped and formed me. I had to accept that my life was not in vain and I was worth value. I built up enough courage to write in the letter that I loved myself and forgave myself for believing all the lies, words, and false narratives about my identity. I forgave myself for all the times of promiscuity and settling for any kind of mistreatment. I wrote how many of my youthful experiences weren't my fault and to stop blaming myself. I wrote how I wasn't stupid nor behaved like a female dog, as I heard those words consistently growing up. I wrote about how unworthy I felt because of all my past choices and failures. I laid out all I could think of and imagine about what was keeping me bound on the legal pad before God. For clarity, this was not a one-time deal or overnight charades. This real work took place when I had the times alone in my dorm room over the course of days, weeks, months, and years. There was always another layer to the onion (me). The stripping, peeling, cutting, rooting out, and then rebuilding, restructuring, and reaffirming took a lot of time.

I also made a commitment to build up my self-esteem and self-confidence with the Lord's guidance and strength. I asked HIM to give me creative ways to express self-love in the midst of my storm. I had my own one-woman empowerment conferences to uplift myself. HE gave me the ideas to write myself other letters every now and then including all the good traits and attributes I liked about me. I wrote lists about my likes and dislikes to really get to know myself. I gave myself birthday cards, wrote words of encouragement on the back of my pictures, and iron-crisped my prison clothes to feel dressed up. I took a manicure class to learn how to do my own nails and remained committed to the process of self-development.

I kept the letter I wrote to myself for a little while. I wanted to reread it as a reminder that I forgave myself, especially on the rough days. Some days required me to speak directly out loud who God said I was from my positive affirmations list I created rather than believing the negative thoughts in my mind. Plus, I combatted negative self-talk by looking up scriptures and memorizing them.

I started getting a couple of responses from the letters I had previously mailed out. One of my family members asked my mom if that was supposed to be some kind of therapy. Neither my mom nor anyone else knew I had written the letters, except those who received them. I chuckled and said, "Yup, it was for me." I wasn't surprised with her response. This particular family member has a long history of never owing up to wrongs regarding anyone. This time, I was able to move past her negativity, letting it fall to the ground rather than placing her thoughts on me.

Another response came in via letter. The individual didn't necessarily take ownership of what he had done per se, but said he was sorry the incidents had happened to me. After reading his letter, I had several thought responses come to mind: 1) Should I second-guess myself to believe I was making the incidents up? 2) Should I take responsibility for his actions? or 3) Should I let this go because this is what toxic behavior looks like and how the lies and false narratives started in the first place? So, I chose the third and added some prayer to it. I was no longer accepting the responsibility to take on someone else's guilt or faults.

During this process, I had the opportunity to attend a three-day retreat sponsored by an outside prison ministry who came into the facility as scheduled. The retreat was held in the auditorium for a selected number of women coming together to get revived. The atmosphere of women supporting other women was astonishing. We gathered in circles and completed multiple activities surrounding unforgiveness. The activity that stood out the most was the one that challenged me to pray, meditate, and write down any area or person(s) that came to mind regarding unforgiveness.

After a small discussion about the topic of unforgiveness, we had to list the situations or people on a piece of paper and fold it up. Just when I thought I had already forgiven everyone or asked for it in return, the Lord revealed another hidden place in my heart. I wrote my list down, trying to hold back tears, and folded it up. Later, a volunteer came by with a trash bag for all of us to throw our unforgiveness lists in. The act in itself resonated with me. Since I'm a pretty visual person, seeing what I had written down be thrown in the trash was enough for me to believe that area was being removed from my heart and placed into the trash where no one could find it, or better yet, into the depths of the sea (see Micah 7:18-19). God's forgiveness gave me the grace to forgive myself and others.

Unforgiveness was the overarching hindrance that had kept me separated from embracing HIS untainted love.

As I continuously yielded to the refining process, I was planted, watered, and pruned as a seed bearing forth new fruit. The more pruning, the more transparent and vulnerable I became before the Lord. My speech started changing from words of guilt or shame to love and acceptance. I was building the relationship with God I so deeply longed for when I prayed that night on my apartment floor in Baltimore letting HIM know I wanted HIM to use me for HIS Glory.

And I knew the changes I desired were happening internally. I could sense it, feel it, and see it when I literally looked in the mirror. My mind was being renewed, my heart cleansed, and my outlook on life was changing. I believed I would be okay for the rest of my incarceration and beyond. I no longer felt the chains of sin and death. I was a new creation, and all the old things had passed away (2 Corinthians 5:17). Everything around me (including my family) was changing, because I had changed. My self-confidence and self-love grew daily.

I started getting positive feedback from the God-appointed officer, Mrs. Kelsey, and my family, and even some of the women on the compound started confiding in me. Someone told me I looked like a beacon of light and another that I sounded different. Their encouragement only allowed me to keep going down my new path. It felt good to know that others were watching without me ever uttering a word. I wasn't looking for glorification. I was embracing redemption and receiving God's loaded benefits in return.

A new page in my life chapter turned. I developed new habits, skills, and thoughts, and gave myself a chance to live a better life. A fresh start.

Chapter 9

Reach Within

Instead of looking for a role model, become the one you want to see.

The level of knowledge and understanding I gained from God's Word was the clarity I needed to understand my true identity. Everything I needed to know about God's untainted love and what that meant concerning me was found there. I had a new walk, a new talk, and new way of thinking. My old way of operating decayed, and a new woman arose. I gained a new strength I never knew I had before. Every positive opportunity that came my way in the facility, I took advantage of, such as becoming the choir director, completing the quick copy apprenticeship building a work ethic, and leading Bible studies and prayer groups.

It felt like a long journey to travel, as I spent close to three years at the maximum-security camp. I had long ago gotten my greens, meaning I switched from a brown dress to a mint green one indicating I was a low-level security risk and could move to a minimum-custody facility. Thankfully, I had no petty write-ups, so I was on track for my projected release date. I decided to stay longer on the compound after I received my greens to complete the quick copy apprenticeship program, which lasted for two years and involved 4,000 hours of training. I thought having this credential might put me at a better advantage when it came time to seek a real job after my release. I would have to work 100x harder than the average job seeker to obtain competitive employment with a felony. I gained some graphic design skills and learned the entire process of printing. During that time, the choir was undergoing some structural changes, and the program director called me to her office, telling me I would be the new choir director. I told her I didn't know a whole lot about music keys and notes, and all that other music theory. She didn't seem to care about my excuses. All the reasons I suggested against it went right over her head and out the window. She talked fast and hurried me out of her office. She smiled, said "I'll see you at rehearsal," and that was that. I did my best to make God and her proud until I had enough. It was a true leadership experience having to step up to the plate and deal with different personalities and behind-the-scenes nonsense.

I took the initiative to hold weekly and monthly Bible studies when the grounds were open. I had a few people show up regularly, and we always tried to end in prayer before count time. I believed this was how God wanted me to spend my time, develop new habits, and share what I was learning in my quiet time with HIM to others. Oftentimes, while my bunkmate was in the dayroom crafting and eating prison-made concoction meals, I was on my bunk pulling out my Bible, legal pad, and a pencil to study. I guess my studying paid off. Other women often came to me for consolation and advice. When I didn't know what to say, I listened, and we prayed about the situation. Dorm E's laundry room and my actual dorm room became houses of prayer when we had a cool, lenient officer on duty. All I can say is that the Lord heard us and answered our prayers.

I was no big shot or celebrity in prison. I was a willing vessel, ready for change, and wanted to share what God had done in me with a small group of others. It was a way of obedience and building my confidence. HE had begun a good work in me (see Philippians 1:6). This became my regular routine. I worked at the duplicating plant five days a week, went to Bible study on Monday nights and weekly choir practice, and completed several continuing education courses to build up my skillset. Fortunately, the academic department offered courses from local colleges, and I took as many courses as were allowed. One class in particular was a game changer for me, taught by one of the wisest women I've ever met in my life, who was also a social worker. Her way of teaching was so dignified and enlightening. She challenged every student in the class to think beyond limiting beliefs and embrace change. She also took the time to speak with me outside of the class, empowering me to accept my uniqueness and become only who God wanted me to be. She called on me to speak in front of the class. In my speech, I charged my classmates to do something different while they were incarcerated and once they got home. I really hoped that at least one person got the message. I was tired of seeing people come back for another stint over and over again while I was serving time for my one bid.

The learning materials from the class propelled me to continue with my personal and self-development progress. I did what I could to improve inside and wrote down my goals for afterwards to keep working on me. I was so proactive that I asked my mom to look up certain information and then mail it to me. My desire to go back to school to finish my degree made the list, among many other ambitious goals.

With time winding down, my apprenticeship training was finally coming to an end. I met all the requirements and had a small graduation in the auditorium. This was the first time I learned about the benefits of delayed gratification. Moving forward, I was confident to believe I would be disciplined enough to hold out for all the goals I wanted to accomplish in my life. Since I was done with the apprenticeship program, I expected to get transferred to another facility any day now. I prepared myself and gave my circles a heads-up. I thought they might send me to Rocky Mount, as this would be the closest facility toward Maryland or New Jersey. Yet, in the middle of the night, I heard a knock on my bunk from the officer telling me I was being transferred to "Little Raleigh," a facility just around the corner. I could've walked there if they let me—that's how close it was. I grabbed my bags and ran softly to Abigail's room. I gave her a hug, told her I was sorry for not spending more time with her, and hurried along. Inside, I was happy and nervous all at once to be moving along. I had less than two years to go with a new outlook on my life.

Little Raleigh was a smaller facility with fewer women. The same rules applied, and the environment was a bit milder. There were four pods and a trailer about 50 feet away from the main facility for the best-behaved women who had outside jobs or attended a degree program. There was a volleyball net on a concrete court, picnic tables, and a small walking path outdoors. My first week on the new compound, I was given an offsite job assignment in the test kitchen. This was a huge deal for me because I hadn't seen what the outside world was like in four years. I had stayed away from watching much television, reading the newspaper, and listening to the local news. Finally, I could look at something besides barbed wire and tall oak trees. Cars rode past honking the horn to tell us what's up, while motorcycles flew by performing tricks. There was a church right across the street along with residential homes. I was transported to and from work by an officer in a dark-tinted white prison van. The test kitchen served state employees and contractors. I ran the stock room, grill, prep station, and cash register on rotations specified by management staff. The simple task of taking out the trash was luxury for scenic purposes. I got to cook and eat real food at the test kitchen. The pay was just enough to get a few hygiene items and snacks from the canteen weekly. A step closer to freedom wasn't too far away.

Once I received my level two privileges, I was able to go out on community passes with a volunteer sponsor to church, retail stores, and home visits as they allowed back then. Getting a volunteer sponsor was kind of the luck of the draw. A specific date and evening time was set by the facility, and individuals would come, meet us in the dayroom area, and go around the room sparking conversation to find a so-called good match. I met with a few different ladies until I hit it off with the right one. From our initial conversation, there was a connection, and we couldn't stop talking to each other. The two hours we had together seemed to go by extremely fast. By the end of our orientation time together, I had a volunteer sponsor. I was thrillful and delighted. My sponsor went above and beyond for me. She introduced me to her family, took me shopping, took me out to eat (with my own money, of course), visited a local park with me, got me connected with a job training center, picked me up for church nearly every Sunday, and treated me like her own daughter. Over the next year and several months, we built an inseparable bond that we still have to this present day.

Being housed at Little Raleigh was certainly better than being at the maximum camp. At the end of the day, though, I never forgot I was in prison. There were some incentives for good behavior that lightened the load a little bit, but I didn't get too comfortable, as the place was incomparable to being in my one-bedroom apartment back home. Here, we still had unannounced locker searches where they threw all of our belongings on the floor searching for contraband, and routine strip searches after having meaningful visits with family or friends. I followed the rules, came back on time from my community passes, and made no AWOL attempts. After work, I usually went to the cafeteria to work out or take a brisk walk. I wrote fewer letters and used the phone a lot more. At Little Raleigh, I got involved in the choir and later on in the dance ministry.

My primary focus remained the same when I transferred. I continued building my relationship with God and improving my self-worth. Other internal challenges arose, but I was able to handle them better. I worked on keeping a positive attitude by not letting anger control me. I dealt with disappointments from others more sensibly. I was given more opportunities in leadership roles at work, the dance ministry, and on the yard. I second-guessed myself from time to time about my worthiness to lead, but I led anyway. I was connected to the Source who guided me.

Shawn had the audacity to write me a letter after I hadn't heard from him in a couple of years. He asked me how I was holding up, telling me he loved me and that he cared. I reread the letter multiple times to be sure I'd read it right. How dare he have the nerve to say all this mushy stuff at a time when I felt like I was ready to move on and he was not on my future radar? Was this the trick to get me to come back to B-more and risk everything all over again? Or did he really mean what he said? Was there another chance for him and me to have a future together and put our pasts behind? My emotions went haywire. My thoughts were perplexed. I fantasized for several days about life with Shawn and what his letter meant.

When I came to my senses and realized confusion doesn't come from God, I wrote Shawn back, telling him how much he didn't love or care for me, how he never wanted to truly be with me. He used me for my loyalty. I described in the letter the attributes of what real love looked like and told him I was moving on—moving further away from the pain, the guilt, heartache, and any memories of him. I threw away his letter to fight against my flesh, as a symbol to press forward to overcome my emotional struggles.

The new year was approaching with no time to waste. I needed to figure out the specifics of my exit plan. "Where should I go?" and "Where would I live?" were among the number of questions that consumed my mind. The big day would be here in no time, a time of rejoicing for sure. I recognized the chance ahead of me to start my life over again, and I wanted to do it right. My sufferings brought out the perseverance in me, along with proven character, which allowed me to have hope because the love of God was poured into my heart through Holy Spirit who was in this season with me (see Romans 5:3-5).

Chapter 10

Moving Forward

**Starting over doesn't mean you've failed
unless you stop trying.**

The new year 2012 rang in while I was outside on the yard during a fire drill. I waited nearly an hour to return back to the trailer so I could get inside from the cold air. The wait didn't seem that long as I gazed upon the stars and thanked God for bringing me into the new year. This would be my final year incarcerated. And not for the whole year, just until four days before the end of July. I was in the home stretch. The seven months remaining would be a piece of cake at this point. My heart and soul burst with gratitude as I reminisced about what life would be like after incarceration. I saw myself excelling, getting a good-paying job and an apartment, going to church, volunteering, and so much more. This would be the continuation of my fresh start. A second chance that so many other women I was leaving behind anticipated. I desired to stay on track and, most of all, please God.

The sounds of some women cheering and others complaining brought me back to my physical reality. I smiled, knowing the time was coming when I no longer had to endure the moaning and grumblings of 30-plus women in one shared space. I would get a good night's sleep not having to wake up to someone talking loudly right next to my head. I would have the opportunity to take as many showers as I wanted in privacy, to use my own personal cellphone and talk for hours if I chose. I would have the freedom to watch sports or whatever else I wanted on TV. Plus, I would be able to choose my preferred style of clothing. I would enjoy and not take for granted all of the privileges I was ready to regain.

After all the buildings were secured and the ruckus subsided, I returned inside the trailer. I couldn't immediately go to sleep because of all the excitement adrenaline. I made small talk with several individuals as we shared our future endeavors. In the back of my mind, I was still toying with the decision of whether to stay in North Carolina or return to New Jersey. Going back to Maryland was out of the picture. If I decided to go home to New Jersey, I would have a guaranteed place to stay, probably find a job more easily, and transportation wouldn't be an issue at all. My real concern with going back to Jersey was the thought of running into old so-called friends or getting involved in the wrong crowd again. I considered it might be a trigger even with a renewed mind. Temptations would come either way, but I wanted to make sure I was following God's leading this time rather than my own. I prayed about it and also made a pros/cons list. I created a transition plan booklet that included Plan A, B, and C. I didn't want to fail, and returning back to prison was NOT an option, so a plan was a must.

Over the next couple of months, I continued to contemplate where to reside after release. One night as I was sitting on the top bunk reading the Bible, I was silently meditating and asking the Lord for direction. As I continued, a scripture verse came to reference. I looked it up, and it spoke about how Joseph named one of his sons Ephraim, meaning *"For God has caused me to be fruitful in the land of my affliction"* (Genesis 41:52). I started thinking about the story of Joseph in full detail. Joseph was stuck in Egypt, the place of his slavery, the country far away from his beloved father, the place where he had languished in prison for years. Yet the Lord made Joseph fruitful in the midst of his suffering ("Fruitful in the Land of Grief"). Eventually, he was released from prison and promoted by Pharoah to be in charge of the whole land of Egypt. By no means did I see myself in Joseph's shoes, considering I was guilty of a crime and he was completely innocent. However, I believed the Lord was speaking directly to me through this scripture. I too would become fruitful in the land of my affliction. After pondering the revelation for several days, I was convinced and filled with peace. North Carolina would become my new home.

Telling my parents was no easy task. They both expected me to move back to New Jersey with their support. I explained to them individually the rationale behind my decision and stood my ground. In their eyes I was still a child, but I had become an adult. The next step was figuring out where I was going to live. During this time, I was taking a reentry life skills class that was supposed to prepare me for reentering society. Most of the topics discussed I had already learned on my own or from a prior class. One of the women teaching the class, who had firsthand experience with the criminal justice system, was working with a new women's transitional home opening up in the local area. She recommended I apply, as I had mentioned to her that I was looking for housing in North Carolina. She even offered to take me out on a community transitional pass to tour the home. A few weeks later, she kept her word, and we headed off to tour the women's transitional home.

The home was located near the downtown area, accessible to the bus line, and in a quiet historic neighborhood. It had a small, well-maintained front yard with a swing on the porch. Inside the home, it was decorative, clean, antique with a Southern modern twist. The downstairs had a private space like a studio apartment for the resident manager along with a dining room area, kitchen, and living room. A piano was available to play in the dining room. The two bedrooms upstairs each held two twin beds, two dressers, and a closet. One of the bedrooms had a really nice-sized bathroom inside of the room with a large vanity and pull-out chair. The atmosphere appeared cozy, welcoming, and warm. As I toured the home, I envisioned myself residing there for a little while. Reality was truly setting in, and I anticipated my freedom. When I headed back to the dorm, I had a peace about the women's transitional home I'd visited and decided to thoroughly complete the application. The application asked a lot of questions regarding my plans for the future. I was easily able to answer every question with honesty, as I had already mapped out everything. Excitedly, I mailed the application packet off to the proper person and prayed I would be accepted. About a month or so went by before I heard anything back. Nevertheless, the good news came right on time. My housing was secured, which was more than half of the battle I would face after starting over.

Since I had worked at a company for nearly four years, learning every single position, I had hoped they would hire me after release. Each time I asked management, they said they were working on it, but nothing had been finalized regarding some kind of contract. The apprenticeship program provided me with a toolkit, so no time was lost. Networking and advocating for myself became natural for me. Gratefully, a number of people were willing to be references for me.

As my search for a job continued, I learned about an organization that supposedly offered second chances to individuals like me. The company had recruiters and employment counselors' positions available. The same woman who took me on a tour to the women's transitional home transported me to the interview. I met the executive director at a fancy hotel. He introduced me to a few team members too. The interview went really well. The guy drilled me with interview questions, but I was well prepared with my responses. The 32-hour job skills training course I took for one week sharpened me for this. At the end of the interview, the executive director extended the job opportunity to me on the spot. He said he felt pretty good about hiring me and that I'd be a great asset on the team for a number of reasons. The stipulation was I had to contact him once I got out, since they didn't have a work release program with the minimum-custody women's facility. There was no written contract; it was basically a verbal agreement. I went back to the facility that day happy like a champion who had just won a boxing match, believing he'd honor the verbal agreement.

Nothing spectacular happened within the last two months of my release. Of course, I was anxious to go any day earlier if I could, but the routine remained—work five days a week, choir practice, dance practice, watch or follow taekwondo videos in the cafeteria, and go on a community pass to church. For some, getting closer to their release dates meant not caring, acting out, and becoming annoyed with anyone in sight. I prayed I wouldn't succumb to those feelings. I wanted nothing to get in my way to delay my release date. Over the course of 5 years and 10 months, I praise God that I never got in a fight, stabbed, beat, raped, or sent to solitary confinement while in prison. Many people have horrific experiences that can occur in that kind of environment, and I believe the hand and favor of God was upon me.

As the weeks and days kept counting down, soon it became my last everything at the facility. My last dinner, my last time sleeping on a hard bunk, my last time using the payphone, and so forth. On the morning of July 26th, it was my last hours on the compound. I got up, read the Bible, stripped the linen from the bunk I was on, got ready, and put on my cute little outfit, a pink button-down denim dress with matching sandals. My dad was on his way from New Jersey to pick me up, which was a blessing. I felt like skipping around Dorm E, but I contained myself to avoid any jealousy or appearing boastful. I made my rounds to all the women with whom I had developed friendships. We gestured our goodbyes through meaningful hugs. My friend Blue and her husband came to visit the week before to take most of my stuff to the home I would soon reside in, so my load on the way out was light. Before lunchtime rolled around, I heard my name over the intercom telling me to report to the control center. I skirted off as fast as I could with my chin and chest up. My once and for all official bag and tag day had come, never to return.

I met my dad outside the secured door of the facility. We embraced for a long time as we were happy to be reunited. This was a testament to the inner work God had done in me concerning my dad, and I was happy to share this moment with him. I asked if he could take a picture of me in front of the building as a reminder of being free, leaving the past behind. I was no longer a ward of the state. No probation officer whatsoever (hard sigh) would come knocking on the door later to supervise me. Thank you, Jesus!

Afterwards, my dad took me to Walmart to purchase my first smartphone. Back in '06, I had flip phone and a Nextel.

It wasn't long before I got the hang of how to operate it. Next, my community sponsor called my dad and asked if we were hungry. We said yes and headed toward IHOP. We got out of the car and headed into the restaurant, and the waitress took me to the designated section my community sponsor was in. As I walked toward the table, my eyes swelled with tears as I saw all the people gathered around. Some people from church and some of my community sponsor's family, all there to celebrate my release. I was overjoyed with all the love and support shown towards me by a group of strangers. Everyone went around the room and spoke about how they knew me or learned about me and spoke encouragement to me. It was a lifegiving experience. I felt encouraged to carry on with my journey. We all ate and laughed. Before we left, my dad rendered some words of appreciation for his baby girl and the whole group prayed for me.

That same day, my dad took me to the women's transitional home where I would reside. He wanted to make sure I would be okay. I told him I was good, knowing I possessed a new level of internal tenacity that I didn't have before. We hugged again and gave kisses to each other on the cheek. I was glad to see someone from my immediate family after release. I didn't get many visits inside because my family was up north; therefore, I was relieved.

When I walked into the house, one of the women I was formerly locked up with was there, and she was happy to see me. She had been waiting for me since she got out in March. Her family lived in another state as well. She and I got along pretty well and were once members of the facility dance ministry team. We shared a room together in the house, and there was one other woman there plus the resident coordinator.

To be honest, it took a while—I'll say a few months—to get mentally adjusted. I longed to be around my family instead of being in a house with three other women. There were house rules, curfews, planned-out weekly schedules, sign-out sheets, and house meetings. One of the women originally on the home's board of directors acted distastefully toward me, questioning why I already had a cellphone. And when Christmastime came around, she was outraged because I came back from New Jersey with a Nook and an iPad, both gifts from my parents, demanding that I return them. I refused, as it wasn't in the house rules. Maybe she thought I would have no family support and saw me as if I were still incarcerated. She was very judgmental and far off course from having a heart to serve women getting out of prison. The folks who oversaw the home expected too much of us. They mandated us to go to life skills class, budgeting class, work, cooking class, sewing class, and two Bible studies a week. We barely had any time to ourselves or personal choice rights. The last straw came when they tried to say my community sponsor couldn't be my mentor, that I would have to choose someone else, or she'd have to go through some kind of extensive training. She had already been mentoring me for almost two years. I couldn't understand what more they wanted. After I endured long months of nonsense from the insane lady and another board member who drove past the house nearly every day to see what we were *not* doing, they were finally relieved of their duties.

I contacted the executive director who had promised to hire me after release. I called numerous times, and when he finally decided to call back, he mentioned that some organizational changes had been made and the opportunity to hire me was no longer available. I was shook and felt rejected. I had high hopes of getting that job, and it would have put me several steps ahead. I talked it over with a couple of people in my support circle. They encouraged me that I would find something else. I wasn't ready to hear NO a thousand times before getting one YES since I had a felony on my record now.

With my networking skills, I was able to reach back out to the organization where I took the 32-hour job skills workshop for job referrals and work with an employment recruiter. She got me a job interview at Golden Corral, a buffet restaurant, as a waitress. The interview went well. I was offered the position making less than minimum wage in the state of North Carolina with tips. I worked Friday through Sunday, 4-8 p.m. The public buses didn't run on Sundays, so I had to take a cab. Every now and then, my coworker, Cara gave me a ride home. Basically, I was paying to go to work because the money I was making went to cab ride fees, not even enough to pay my $400 rent at the transitional home. I did what I had to do for two months. Then, I contacted the employment recruiter to see if something else was available, explaining to her my economic situation. Through my steady persistence, she contacted me back again with another opportunity as a housekeeper at a country club. The interviewer was pretty nonchalant, only asking questions about my availability and if I knew how to clean. I attempted to give him my criminal background story spiel and how I deserved a second chance, but that wasn't necessary; he hired me on the spot, adjusting my work schedule from Tuesday through Saturday 2:30-10 p.m., like the other second-shift staff, to Wednesday through Saturday 12:30-10:30 p.m. so I could continue with the nine-month life skills program I had already started, which required my attendance every Tuesday evening. This meant I worked four days a week for 10-hour shifts with full-time benefits. It was a pretty sweet deal, I thought. I had three days to rest, run errands, and attend class. My co-workers didn't understand why I had such a unique shift since I had just started, but it was none of their business for me to explain the favor I'd received. I worked at the country club for about a year and a half. I cleaned bathrooms and shower rooms, tennis and fitness buildings, operated commercial laundry equipment, and washed hundreds of dirty linens. The job wasn't beneath me. It was a chance to build up my work ethic and gain character and job references, while leveraging and learning new skills on my days off.

Right before I switched to another position with a different company, I was able to get my own car. My mentor, formerly my volunteer sponsor, had allowed me to use her personal vehicle to take the driver's test several months prior. My previous driver's license had expired in the state of New Jersey, so I had to take the written and road tests all over again. I took my picture in my work uniform that day, and I drove to work with my mentor in the passenger seat. That spring, I purchased a used vehicle with no car payments attached. It allowed me to accept another job opportunity a month later with more pay while commuting a little farther away.

The job opportunity doors that opened up have been blessings upon blessings. There are some employers who appreciate honesty and value giving job seekers a second chance no matter the story. And I can't front, knowing somebody who knows somebody always helps too. As I started to be successful with reentering society, I still had other emotional challenges that needed to be dealt with. There was still the pressing thought of seeing Shawn again and potentially being reunited. For three days in a row, I attempted to contact him at his mom's house with no answer. I left messages, and he never returned my calls. After the third time, I had a fit on my bedroom floor, crying and sobbing as if I grieved for someone. That was the last time I attempted to connect with him ever again in my life. I was set free from any emotional ties with him.

Unfortunately, this didn't stop me from meeting new snakes. There was a guy at the country club, day after day, who would come to my work area to talk to me. I could see from afar that he would be trouble. However, during a period of loneliness, I convinced myself I could possibly convert him to getting "saved." I thought I was strong enough to play the game without sexual activity. He gave me rides home from work, and most times I just teased him by letting him take a peek at my thighs or give me a goodnight kiss. We made plans to meet up at a hotel before Valentine's Day to link up. The night went as planned, but I later learned it wasn't worth it. After all the trash I found out about him, I immediately left him alone, all while still praying to God to help me overcome this mess I kept finding myself in. Eventually, he got fired at work, so I no longer had to see him there. I ignored all his calls and texts.

On top of that, one would think I would have finally learned my lessons: 1) Stop looking for love in all the wrong places, and 2) Don't hook up with people at work. Number 2 used to be a rule I lived by, but I think desperation, loneliness, and not being with a man for almost six years had my nose wide open. For that reason, I started watching some eye candy at the country club. He appeared well mannered, respectful, and nice looking. He worked temporarily at the country club for special fine dining events, big parties, and weddings. The conversation was casual, a mild flirtation that carried over to a friendship and then a relationship lasting for two and a half years. We were completely opposite. I was an ambitious go-getter with set goals, and he was a whining bartender who constantly complained about his jobs. He held four different jobs during our relationship, always quitting before finding another one. He claimed to be spiritual, but we never went to church together. For a while I let it ride, compromising my own values and beliefs. I stopped going to church for two years, despite knowing it was the lifeline I needed to stay the course.

I left the transitional home after 13 months, then moved into a shared living space situation for about the same length of time, and eventually found my own apartment. I let a coworker talk me into allowing this man to move in with me. I worked and went to school full-time majoring in Human Services, and she convinced me that I could save money and pay less expenses if he moved in. Foolishly, I accepted the idea and presented it to him. At this time, he was struggling to pay his own rent for $500/month, utilities included, which was already a warning sign. I had never lived with a guy before. Noted, it was the most miserable 10 months, too. This guy could barely pay $300 every month toward rent, and he didn't have any barriers like I did. He made more than a few excuses.

I thought I could put up with him, because overall he was a nice, easygoing, respectful person, until one December around the holidays, when my mom came to visit. Her presence around the apartment must have ruffled his feathers. He became quiet and distant. Finally, I asked him what was wrong. He broke down crying, saying that couldn't do this (the relationship) anymore, that he didn't want to hurt me because he didn't know if he wanted to get married or have any kids with me. He said he was never going to go to church and saw how I truly cared about it. When he told me all this, I was not hurt at all. I realized how I barely thought about him in everyday life and having him get out of my apartment would be a joy. I was grateful my mom came to visit and the Lord used her to reveal what both he and I needed to see.

As the days went on, I remember going into the bathroom and crying on my knees, telling God how sorry I was for being in this relationship and being disobedient. I told HIM how I wanted to live right and not be subjugated to men. I asked for forgiveness and a greater strength to make better choices and learn to be celibate. I heard the voice of the Lord say, *I am with you, I am with you.* As I heard these soothing words over and over, I received comfort and peace. I believed what I heard and didn't feel condemned. When I picked myself up off the bathroom floor, I had the courage to tell the guy I was dating that he needed to move out as soon as possible—and no more sex. From that point on, he slept in the spare bedroom until the day he left my apartment. In the meantime, I got reconnected to my church family, admitted my struggles to my mentor, and took some discipleship classes. It felt good to stand up for what I knew to be right and say no. This helped to build my self-confidence and understand my value as a woman, what I should and shouldn't accept. I stopped chasing after approval and seeking attention. I became content with being single. Through much prayer, spending time with God, and continuous internal work, I accepted the purpose and plans the Lord had in store for me (see Jeremiah 29:11).

Chapter 11

Untainted Love

It's time for you to reclaim your self-worth through God's Untainted Love.

I asked myself numerous times on this journey, "Does God love me? If HE loved me so much, why did I have to live a hard life of pain and suffering so young? Why was I abused? Why did I have to grow up in such misery? Why did I end up in prison for a long time when so many others got away? Where was my secret pass that others received to scurry through life with no worries or bad happenings?" And there was only one answer I could find. No matter what, through the good, bad, ugly, and indifferent in my life, God loved me. He always had and always will. God's protection surrounded me in spite of every challenge, and even when I made poor decisions when I knew it was wrong, His grace and mercy followed me. His love remained untainted toward me, and I found rest in that.

For the person who may know in your heart that God has called you and chosen you—don't give up. Ask HIM for strength and wisdom, and take heed to ways of escape HE has provided regarding your situations. Even if you feel like you may have messed up or fallen from grace, so to speak, God is near and hears you when you call out to HIM for help. Just be honest with God. HE is so persistent toward us, and we must be persistent toward HIM too.

This journey has been one heck of a ride. It's been a fight. And most definitely, there have been some victories. I wouldn't be the person I am today without the untainted love of God. I'm deeply grateful to God for how far I've come. Through His untainted love, my journey of building self-confidence, seeing my true worth in Christ, and inner healing continues.

All my life experiences have taught me valuable lessons. Today I'm proud of who I am and what God has done in and through me. I'm stronger, wiser, bolder, and most importantly surrounded with the Father's untainted love. Through this memoir, may you be moved to continue on your own journey toward healing and increasing your self-worth. If you haven't recognized the true, pure love that comes from God, I encourage you to ask God to show it to you, for it to consume you and bring an overflow of His untainted love that eradicates all your hurts, failures, pain, and sins.

LESSONS ON THE JOURNEY

Here are 10 lessons I've learned that I'd personally like to leave with you:

1. *Don't make excuses for the ones who hurt you.*

I had to remind myself not to make excuses for the ones who hurt me. I wasn't accountable for their actions. I think as women, sometimes we can question or blame ourselves for any type of abuse, thinking that it's somehow our fault. Not so! So what if you're pretty, have a nice smile, cute body, great personality, or whatever else? It is not a warrant for entry by any means.

2. *Forgiveness starts with me.*

It's when I forgave myself of all the shame, guilt, and filth that I felt and decided to forgive others that the inner healing truly began. Of course, it wasn't easy to forgive, but I realized this was where my freedom lay. I believed God would help me get through it. Once I stopped beating myself up for everything in my past and removed the focus on how others mistreated me, and I became restless, I was able to break FREE from all the yokes around my neck (see Genesis 27:40).

3. *Speak up, let your voice be heard to God and before others.*

I was a very shy and quiet person. For years, I kept everything I was going through bound up on the inside of me. I started talking to God as a confidant, telling him how I felt, how I saw myself, and what I needed from him. God gave me the strength and courage to speak up, come forward about my traumas, and share the truth with trusted counselors and my parents. *"If we confess our sins, he is faithful and just to forgive us our sins and to cleanse us from all unrighteousness"* (1 John 1:9).

4. *Loving yourself is an ongoing journey after experiencing adverse childhood traumatic experiences or other trauma-related events.*

The process of learning to love yourself doesn't happen overnight. It is a lifelong journey, and it gets better as long as you stay committed, stay removed from toxic people/situations, and give yourself time to heal.

5. *Seek wise counseling and/or help from professionals anytime you feel it's necessary.*

Neglecting sound wisdom and unsought counseling can be detrimental to one's healing progress. There's no shade in speaking with a loved one. However, we can lean more so on the opinions or views of our family and friends rather than discussing the whole truth with someone who won't hold any judgment. You can have the opportunity for someone to really listen to you and gain additional support/feedback for how to make the necessary changes in your life that *you* decide (see Proverbs 11:14 and 15:22).

6. *My self-worth and image are untarnished in the eyes of Father God through His Son Jesus Christ and through*

the revealing of Holy Spirit by the Word of God.

It was through my traumatic experiences that I saw a distortion of my worth when I looked in the mirror. God never saw my self-worth tarnished or damaged. He always viewed me as His own, as His daughter, loved, beautiful, worthy, and unblemished (see Genesis 1:26-27, 31; Isaiah 43:1-7; Romans 8:1-17).

7. *No one gets to choose the consequences of their bad choices.*

I thought I was going to get some kind of big break by not having to do any time, or that a miracle would happen to make my sentence much shorter. I used to wonder in bitterness why others in similar situations never got caught, but I did. Then I realized I had no control over the outcome of my bad decisions. I only had the option to woman up and take responsibility for my actions.

8. *The Word of God "is a lamp to my feet and a light to my path" (Psalm 119:105).*

Over the years, I have relied on the Word of God to teach and lead me daily. Through my darkest hours, it has brought me through snares and thorns and allowed me to remain consistent in my daily walk with God. I can't live a purposeful life without it.

9. *"God has not given us a spirit of fear, but of power and*

of love and or a sound mind" (2 Timothy 1:7).

This scripture gives me the confidence and reassurance I need to keep moving forward with my destiny. Many of my fears paralyzed me until I took steps to overcome them, including writing this book. All fears don't typically just go away, but please know a *spirit* of fear (constant operation of it) is NOT from God.

10. *Pray with ACTION.*

Let your prayers be heard to God, and make sure to listen up so you can hear from Him. Hearing His voice will lead you toward the actions you need to take concerning what you're praying about.

Closing Prayer

Dear Reader,

As you travel down your own road toward self-love, forgiveness, and freedom, I want to intercede on your behalf to pray that you endure the process and never give up if you desire to be healed.

So, in the name of Jesus...

I pray a release to the weight of condemnation as it is not from God. I declare over you that God has not given you a spirit of condemnation nor a spirit of fear to possess. I speak love, healing, and hope to your entire being. I pray that you will see you have been made in the image of God, and because you have been made in the image of God, you have the rights and access to His untainted love. I pray you will be captivated and drawn toward His love rather than seeking the love and approval of fallible people.

I speak You are Free. You are Loved. Let every generational curse of abandonment, fear, rejection, self-pity, self-sabotage, and self-neglect, as well as word curses, be broken and stripped from you in Jesus' Name. I pray you will mount up on wings like eagles to regain your power and strength to fight for the life God originally intended for you. I pray you will experience an abundance of peace and comfort during your own healing process. I pray you will be able to stand against the wiles and temptations of the devil. To say no to predators and individuals appearing as angels of light to come distract and disrupt, to have a keen eye for individuals who come and try to take you off course.

Be Free in Jesus' Name. I pray you will have supernatural courage and strength and that you will be guided by Holy Spirit to do what is right and accept the will of the Lord for your life. May your soul prosper, may your emotions be healed in Jesus' Name. Let no mental turmoil overtake you and overrule you, but stand confidently knowing the Lord is with you and HE is *for* you! May any curses or acts of perversion be broken off of you in Jesus' Name. Let purity and celibacy be your portion if that's the season you're in. I pray you will be restored, that your inner being will be restored, that you will walk in Wholeness. In Jesus' Mighty Name, Amen.

Notes

The Bible, English Standard Version.

Bradford, Kate. "Reducing the Effects of Adverse Childhood Experiences." *LegisBrief*, vol. 28, no. 29, August 2020, https://www.ncsl.org/research/health/reducing-the-effects-of-adverse-childhood-experiences.aspx

"Fruitful in the Land of Grief." *Theology of Work*, https://www.theologyofwork.org/the-high-calling/daily-reflection/fruitful-land-grief

"*Operation* (game)." *Wikipedia*, https://en.wikipedia.org/wiki/Operation_(game)

Sacks, Vanessa, and David Murphey. "The Prevalence of Adverse Childhood Experiences, Nationally, by State, and by Race or Ethnicity." *Child Trends*, February 12, 2018, https://www.childtrends.org/publications/prevalence-adverse-childhood-experiences-nationally-state-race-ethnicity

"What's Your Concept of Trauma?" *Crisis Prevention Institute,* https://www.crisisprevention.com/Blog/SAMHSA-Concept-of-Trauma

"Words from Prison: Did You Know...?" *ACLU,* https://www.aclu.org/other/words-prison-did-you-know